# LATIN AMERICA
## AND THE
# ENLIGHTENMENT

# LATIN AMERICA
## AND THE
# ENLIGHTENMENT

*Second Edition*

ESSAYS BY
ARTHUR P. WHITAKER,
ROLAND D. HUSSEY, HARRY BERNSTEIN,
JOHN TATE LANNING, ALEXANDER MARCHANT,
*and* CHARLES C. GRIFFIN

INTRODUCTION BY FEDERICO DE ONÍS

EDITED BY ARTHUR P. WHITAKER

# GREAT SEAL BOOKS
*A Division of Cornell University Press*

ITHACA, NEW YORK

## PREFATORY NOTE

ORIGINALLY published in 1942, this little book has long been out of print. Despite the fact that its publication apparently stimulated, and in any case was followed by, a great increase in the volume of historical writing on various aspects of its central theme, it still remains the only compact account of the subject. Also, although the subsequent flood of publication on the subject has added many new details and brought about some change of interpretation and emphasis, most of the main conclusions of the original essays are as valid today as when they were first stated two decades ago.

It is doubtless for these reasons that there has been an increasing demand in recent years that the book be made more easily available. This edition differs from the original in the addition of a select list of books and articles published since 1941 and an index (lacking in the original) and the substitution of a new preface and a new concluding essay by Charles C. Griffin in place of the one by the late Arthur Scott Aiton, "The Spanish Government and the Enlightenment in America." The other five original essays, and the introduction by

[ v ]

the late Federico de Onís, are reproduced here precisely as they first appeared.

The decision to replace the original concluding essay with a new one was adopted in view of the principal change of historical outlook that has taken place since 1942. One major component of the change, as described in a recent letter to me from one of the contributors, John Tate Lanning, was "a shift to Descartes and Newton as the start of the Enlightenment" and away from blind faith in the influence of Rousseau, Voltaire, and the French generation of 1789 as "the sole basis of the awakening that led to the Latin American wars of independence." This and the other components are ably described in Professor Griffin's new essay, which should make it clear to any attentive reader that the Enlightenment in Latin America was much more than a mere preparation for the anti-colonialism and political independence movement of the early nineteenth century.

For aid in updating the bibliography, I am much indebted to the surviving contributors to the original volume, Harry Bernstein, John Tate Lanning, and Alexander Marchant, and also to Irving A. Leonard, Eugenio Pereira Salas, of Santiago, Chile, and Silvio Zavala, of Mexico and Paris. I note with sorrow that among the original authors death has taken not only Arthur Scott Aiton but also Roland D. Hussey, whose essay "Traces of French Enlightenment in Colonial Hispanic America" is one of the chief ornaments of this re-issue, as it was of the original volume. I wish to renew my original expression of gratitude to William E. Lingelbach, general editor of the series of Appleton-Century Historical Essays in which this book first appeared, and to the Carnegie Endowment for International Peace, which aided in its publication.

ARTHUR P. WHITAKER

*University of Pennsylvania*
*April 10, 1961*

# INTRODUCTION

THE excellent essays which make up this volume have in common not only the subject matter but the spirit which informs them. There is in all of them a generous, affirmative intention which may be considered typically American. The method they use is to seek the truth in the broadest, most just and comprehensive interpretation of the facts, leaving aside all accepted prejudices.

The eighteenth century in Europe showed a lack of understanding and impartiality in judging Spain and her history, and these essays correct the errors of that interpretation while, at the same time, affirming the positive values and the universal influence of the ideas created by that century. Without prejudice or partiality toward any European nationality, they make manifest the part played by France, Germany, and England in the total process of European Enlightenment and its influence in Spanish and Portuguese America. This latter is given the same attention as the former, and is evaluated in its individual and typical characteristics, not merely included, as so often happens, in an exclusive or predominantly Spanish American conception, where it is either lost sight of or treated as an appendage. Neither do they play up to limited nationalistic concepts of Hispano-America, in which the knowledge of one country often leads to blindness toward the others, with the result that the total vision of the unity of Hispanic American civilization, and, within this unity, of the rich diversity of its national forms, is lost. These essays likewise correct the mutual lack of understanding that has so often existed between Spain and Spanish America, and they never uphold the one at the expense of the other; on the contrary, they are clearly aware of the relation and parallelism between them.

In this spirit and with this method these essays have succeeded in outlining in clear, precise fashion the period which, after the Conquest, is without question the most important in the historical development of Spanish and Portuguese America. As a rule, the two periods which have received the most attention are the Colonial, which was but a consequence of the Conquest, and that of the Independence, which was but a consequence of the crisis of the eighteenth century. During this century there took place in America a new development which has repeated itself to our own day throughout the diverse phases of modern history: the confrontation of the European culture of that time with the Hispanic tradition which had been in force since the sixteenth century. This was the case in America as well as in the Peninsula. The consequence for both was the awakening of a number of select spirits to the consciousness of the gulf which had developed between Hispanic civilization and that which had come into being during the two preceding centuries of rivalry, strife and isolation. From this moment the Hispanic peoples are to regard both their past and their future in a new light.

The eighteenth century represented the triumph and general acceptance of the modern progressive system of thought on which the new conception of Europe was based. Outside of this conception of normal Europe there remained many European things, among these the Hispanic nations, the off-spring and heirs of a culture which was at variance in many of its postulates and aims to that which had triumphed in Europe and which was consequently to chart the course of history. In those very nations which were the creators and masters of this modern Europe—France, England, Germany—the ideology of the Enlightenment, on which it was founded, had to struggle with the forces of the past which they bore within themselves and which had been in conflict with the new tendencies ever since the Renaissance. The crisis, however, was much sharper in the Hispanic nations, where to the rivalry between the old and the new there was added the fact that the new came to be identified with what was foreign and the old, with the national.

The development and the effects of this new historic process, of the contact between these two spiritually contradictory worlds, and their accommodation and concordance within the Hispanic mind and institutions are studied with care and penetration in these essays. The special character of this century, known as that of "enlightened despotism," made it possible to carry out this difficult process of adjustment and solution of the crisis with singular success because those involved were select minorities and exceptional individuals. The Hispanic genius has always felt at home in those moments of conflict which have fostered the development of the individual, and has always been attracted to problems difficult or even impossible of solution. This is why so many and such gifted reformers arose in Spain, in Portugal, and in Hispanic America in the eighteenth century. As they became aware of the distance which history had created between modern European and traditional Hispanic culture, they made heroic efforts to bridge the gap, even though, in certain aspects, it was an abyss they had to cross.

The effects of this ideological leaven of the eighteenth century in the nineteenth, consequences of such magnitude as the Independence of Spanish and Portuguese America and the formation of their new nationalities, are not studied in these essays as they fall without the chronological limits of the epoch with which the essays deal. Everywhere those optimistic, humanitarian, abstract ideals of the Enlightenment as they spread through the other strata of society brought about the great historical transformations of the nineteenth century which were accompanied by conflict, revolution, and civil wars of varying intensity in the different countries. In the Hispanic world, in both America and Europe, the struggle between the forces of tradition and the new ideas has been more violent, more complex, and more difficult of solution than anywhere else.

There was on this continent a country, the United States, which represented the American flowering, and, therefore, a living example for the Hispanic Americans, of this new conception of life which had been growing in them since the eighteenth century. The light these essays shed on the important rôle played by the United States in the spiritual transformation of Hispanic America in the eighteenth century lends them special interest. They reveal that the intellectual relations between the Americas are not an invention of our day, as many believe. Ever since the seventeenth century, both in this America and the other, there have been many people who have realized the importance of maintaining these relations, with a deep awareness of American solidarity.

FEDERICO DE ONÍS

*Columbia University*

# CONTENTS

[ xv ]

# LATIN AMERICA AND THE
ENLIGHTENMENT

# THE DUAL RÔLE OF LATIN AMERICA
# IN THE ENLIGHTENMENT

*By* Arthur P. Whitaker

Designed to serve merely as an introduction to the other essays in this volume, the present essay sketches the two rôles that Latin America played simultaneously in relation to the Enlightenment, namely, the active rôle of participant in that movement and the passive rôle of object lesson or horrible example in the writings of its leading exponents in Europe.

An excellent starting-point for this discussion is provided by Carl Becker's brilliant little book, *The Heavenly City of the Eighteenth-Century Philosophers.* Although Mr. Becker's book is naturally concerned primarily with Europe, it contains some stimulating remarks on the rôle of Latin America in the Enlightenment and furnishes a background against which the present discussion may be projected.

According to Mr. Becker, the Enlightenment in its early stages made a cult of reason; but it became increasingly apparent that reason would not reveal the universal principles of right and wrong, the scale of values, necessary to justify the reforms which the philosophers wished to effect. This logical dilemma led them to assume that they already had what they needed—the intellectual security and assured knowledge in the light of which they could confidently interpret the past experience of mankind and build its future on the basis of the natural goodness and perfectibility of man. So, he concludes, the eighteenth-century Philosophers, like the medieval scholastics, were engaged in the "nefarious enterprise of reconciling the facts of experience with truths already, in some fashion, revealed to them"—in short, the Enlightenment was "an eighteenth-century search for the Holy Grail." But he is well aware that it was a very special kind of Holy Grail for which they were searching, for he points out that from the middle of the century the promotion of useful knowledge—the knowledge of such subjects as commerce, agriculture, history, and morality—was an increasingly important feature of the Enlightenment.

Mr. Becker makes very few explicit applications of these ideas to Latin America. He discusses only one of its two rôles—its passive rôle—and he devotes only one long passage to this topic. This is the passage in which he uses Abbé Raynal's *Histoire des Indes* to illustrate how aboriginal America, together with China, was used by the Philosophers to prove the natural goodness of man by showing how noble the savage was before he was corrupted by the European society which the philosophers were seeking to reform.

Except for a few passing references, that is all that Mr. Becker said about Latin America, and it is all that needed to be said for his purpose, since his main concern was with the Enlightenment at its center in France, Germany, and England, and with the development of its guiding ideas. Our present concern, on the other hand, is with the Enlightenment in a part of the periphery of the European world (the Iberian countries and their American colonies) and with the way in which this region received, used, and modified the ideas of the Enlightenment.

From this point of view there are three general considerations about the Enlightenment in Europe that should be kept in mind in the following discussion. In the first place, looking back at the eighteenth century through the lurid glow of the French Revolution, we are inclined to regard the Enlightenment as, consciously or unconsciously, essentially revolutionary in the political and social sense. This may be the truth, but it is certainly not the whole truth, for in one of its most important aspects—its zeal for the promotion of useful knowledge—the Enlightenment was ardently supported in circles

[ 5 ]

that were politically and socially conservative. Indeed, useful knowledge was often promoted for the very purpose of fortifying the political and social status quo. This is important for our purpose, because it was in this aspect that the Enlightenment reached its highest development in the Ibero-American world. In the second place, we should stress the progress of the Enlightenment in Germany and Italy because of their close relations with eighteenth-century Spain. This is especially true of the important part played by Germany in promoting useful knowledge in Europe and the whole Hispanic world in the second half of the eighteenth century. In the third place, we should note that the progress and diffusion of the Enlightenment was in large measure due to special institutes and academies, such as the Royal Society of London and the Academy of Sciences of Paris. This is particularly important because the universities were for the most part indifferent if not hostile to the Enlightenment and, in fact, did not then carry on the research activities which were so necessary to the promotion of useful knowledge.

These general remarks will, I hope, make it easier to appreciate the dual rôle of Latin America in relation to the Enlightenment.

To begin with the passive rôle of Latin America —its rôle as Exhibit A in the chamber of horrors of the Philosophers: Mr. Becker's choice of Raynal's *Histoire des Indes* to illustrate this point was a happy one for his purpose, for Raynal's book did express the opinion of the Philosophers about Latin America as well as the rest of the Indies, and it also contributed greatly towards disseminating and strengthening their opinion, since it was immensely popular, passing through 54 editions before 1800, and was well described by a contemporary, Horace Walpole, as "the Bible of two worlds." But the Enlightenment had already run more than half its course when the first edition of the book was published in 1770; and we may well ask what the Philosophers thought about Latin America in the long years before the publication of Raynal's best-seller, and from what sources they obtained their ideas about it.

The answer to the first question seems to be that Raynal contributed little that was new. He merely served up familiar ideas in a more entertaining and striking way, and that was doubtless why his book was so popular. This is the answer that one might have expected. The answer to the second question, however, may be rather surprising, for it is that the portrait of Latin America painted by the Philosophers before Raynal and only retouched by him was in turn merely a revised edition of the Black Legend sketched in the sixteenth century by the Spaniard

Bartolomé de las Casas and elaborated by many willing hands in other countries in the seventeenth century. Are we, then, to conclude that the eighteenth-century Philosophers had nothing essentially new to say on this, one of their favorite themes? Perhaps; but at least they put the familiar portrait to a new use—and that was all that really mattered, for, as Mr. Becker has told us, the Enlightenment prided itself not so much on its ideas as on the use it made of them.

From this point of view, the Enlightenment does mark a new and peculiarly interesting stage in the history of the Black Legend. In its first stage, its founder, Las Casas, had used it to discredit secular government in America in order to establish the control of the Church over it. In the second stage, the Legend had been exploited by the foreign enemies of Spain, among whom many were Protestants seeking to discredit Roman Catholicism. Now, in the third stage, the philosophers of the Enlightenment used the Black Legend as a weapon in their assault on all revealed religion, Protestant as well as Roman Catholic; in other words, reversing the purpose of its founder, Las Casas, and broadening its field of action, they employed the Legend to discredit ecclesiastical power and establish secular power in unchallenged control of human affairs throughout their world.

It is from this standpoint that we can best appreciate the Enlightenment's unflattering portrait of Spain and its régime in America. The fundamental assumption of the painters was that the Spanish Empire was a stronghold of the ecclesiasticism and obscurantism with which they were contending everywhere. This assumption was never shaken in the eighteenth century, not even by the expulsion of the Jesuits from the Spanish Empire in 1767, a measure which was carried out in the spirit of the Enlightenment by its sympathizers—Conde de Aranda and others—in Spain. Raynal's *Histoire des Indes,* which was published only three years later, moderated none of the severity of the Enlightenment's judgment on the Spaniards, whether they lived in Europe or America, and it fixed that judgment firmly in the mind of Europe for many years to come.

This was a poor reward to the Spaniards for the services they were rendering to the Enlightenment. These were important, as were also, though in less degree, those of the Portuguese, and in both cases the services were rendered by Iberians in America as well as in Europe.

This brings us to the second rôle of Latin America, its positive rôle as a participant in the Enlightenment. Much of what needs to be said on this subject can be omitted here because it will be brought out in the following essays; but there are some general observations that it would be well for me to make since they may provide a useful framework for the subsequent discussion. I wish to preface these observations with the warning that they give a very different view of the Enlightenment from that contained in Menéndez y Pelayo's account of it in his classic *Heterodoxos españoles,* in which he describes the Enlightenment (which he significantly calls *"Enciclopedismo"*) as due almost entirely to French influence, as simply an outgrowth of French "impiety" and regalist Jansenism, as almost exclusively an anti-clerical movement, as possessing substantially the same character in the Portuguese world as in the Spanish world, and as static throughout the eighteenth century.

The first of my general observations is that Brazil's reception of the Enlightenment was different from that of Spanish America, and as the eighteenth century wore on, the two regions seemed to be developing along divergent lines. For reasons that we cannot enter into here, Brazil was less responsive than Spanish America to the Enlightenment; and according to Gilberto Freyre, it was developing an increasingly Asiatic character and that process was arrested only by the establishment of the political independence of Brazil, which brought it back into the main stream of occidental civilization.

At the beginning of the Enlightenment, there was little reason to expect this divergence between Brazil and Spanish America, for just as the movement was getting well under way in its chief centers, France and England, these two powers gained positions of great influence in the Iberian peninsula— France in Spain, and England in Portugal; but the new seed found a more fertile soil in Spain than in Portugal. To be sure, Spain was not a country in which a prudent man would attack established institutions, either political or religious; but, as we have seen, there were aspects of the Enlightenment which even a strict political and religious conformist could cultivate, and some of them had a special interest for Spain. Las Casas himself was a Spaniard, and since his time Spanish humanitarianism had been directed particularly towards those noble savages, the American Indians, who were the objects of a major cult of the Enlightenment. The Spaniards were, moreover, acutely conscious at this time of the sad decline of their country's prestige and power since the days of Philip II and were therefore receptive to new ideas, even to ideas of political and religious reform, so long as these could be carried out within the framework of the established order. They were particularly responsive to the newer aspect of the Enlightenment—the zeal which it developed for the promotion of useful knowledge. The benefits of this were sorely needed on both sides of the Atlantic—for example, to revive the languishing production of gold, silver, and mercury mines.

For these and other reasons, Spain responded readily to the stimulus of the Enlightenment with a notable scientific revival, the organization of many academies and institutes, and the production of a long line of books that breathe the spirit of the Enlightenment and many of which still enjoy international esteem. These works range all the way from the early eighteenth-century writings of the prolific and encyclopedic Padre Benito Feijóo, who was acclaimed in one of the chief journals of the French Enlightenment, the *Mémoires de Trévoux,* to the late eighteenth-century *Cartas Marruecas* of Cadalso, which has frequently been compared to Montesquieu's *Lettres Persanes.* To Spanish America the movement found its way mainly through the writings of Spanish authors, such as Feijóo, whom contemporary Peruvians regarded as one of the greatest geniuses of the modern age, and through Spanish scientists and travelers such as Antonio de Ulloa of Seville and José Celestino Mutis of Cádiz. It also found its way there through French and German scientists and travelers, such as Charles de la Condamine and Alexander von Humboldt. How it flowed back from

Spanish America to Spain is illustrated by the case of the Peruvian Pablo Olavide, of melancholy renown, which time does not permit me to recount here.

The other general observations I wish to make are that, in the matter of the promotion of useful knowledge, it was not so much from France or England as from Germany that Spain and Spanish America were enlightened in the latter part of the age; and that in this transfer of ideas a highly important rôle was played by those special academies and institutes which, as we have seen, grew up beside the universities and in the eighteenth century performed many of the research functions which have subsequently been taken over in large part by the universities.

One example will have to suffice for both of these observations. About 1760 an academy of natural sciences was organized by the Conde de Peñaflorida at the town of Azcoitia in the Basque country—a region in which the upper classes were in closer cultural contact with France than with Madrid, and in which more copies of the French *Encyclopédie* were sold than in any other part of Spain. In true "philosophical" fashion, this academy ranged far and wide in its discussions, which, with the zeal of the Enlightenment, were held every day in the week: on Mondays, the subject of discussion was mathematics; on Tuesdays, physics; on Wednesdays, history; on Thursdays and Sundays, music; and on Fridays and Saturdays, current events. In 1766 this academy was converted, under the patronage of the King's chief Minister, Grimaldi, into the *Sociedad de Amigos del País.* When the Jesuits were expelled the following year, it quickly obtained possession of one of their colleges, and established in it the soon famous *Semanario de Vergara,* which was a center of anti-clerical instruction and "materialistic" studies, and the first secular school ever established in Spain. Encouraged by its success and by the protection afforded it by the court, liberals all over Spain promptly established similar societies—about 40 in all—at Madrid, Valencia, Seville, and elsewhere.

So far, the French influence seems to have been predominant, but that of Germany was soon to appear. In 1785 two Spaniards, the Elhuyar brothers, Fausto and Juan José, who had been studying pure and applied science with the support of the *Sociedad Vascongada de Amigos del País* and had already studied in France and Germany, were sent to Germany again by the Spanish Court. They studied at the famous school of mines at Freiberg, Saxony; and on orders from Madrid, one of the brothers, Fausto de Elhuyar, organized two missions of German scientists and miners for service in America, one in Mexico and the other in Peru.

The mission to Mexico, composed partly of Germans, was led by Fausto de Elhuyar himself. He remained there for a quarter of a century, and, as Alexander von Humboldt testified, rendered important services in promoting the natural sciences in Mexico as well as in his primary task of improving mining methods in that country. Similarly, the other mission, composed entirely of Germans and led by the Saxon Baron von Nordenflicht, spent some twenty years in Peru and gave an impulse to scientific studies there, through the *Sociedad de Amantes del País* of Lima, through personal contact with notable Peruvians such as José Hipólito Unánue, and through the individual efforts of some of the members of the mission, such as Thaddeus Haenke, a Sudeten German scientist, who spent the rest of his life in useful labor in South America.

Thus, when in the closing years of the century the German Alexander von Humboldt went to Spanish America to begin the long residence that was to furnish the material for his classic accounts of that region, he was only following in the footsteps of many of his fellow countrymen. And it is to be noted that, although Humboldt was the spiritual heir of the philosophers, personal acquaintance with Spanish America emancipated him from their stock ideas about it, and he painted a portrait of it that was perhaps more generous than just, but which was at any rate strikingly different from the stereotype popularized by Raynal, and different mainly because it presented Spanish American culture in a far more favorable light. Humboldt's case shows that Latin America's active rôle as participant in the Enlightenment was at last altering its passive rôle as an exhibit in the case prepared by the Philosophers; but the change had been too long delayed, for by the time Humboldt's new portrait was completed, the waters of the Enlightenment had run out in the marshes of war and revolution.

The German stimulus to Spanish science, the missions of Elhuyar and Nordenflicht to Mexico and Peru, and the work of Humboldt are only a few illustrations of the ferment that the Enlightenment was causing in the Spanish Empire in the last days of the old régime, a ferment that was encouraged by the Spanish government itself. Many other illustrations might be given. For example, in Spanish America, Cartesianism was undermining scholasticism and drawing the lines of thought that were to be followed through the struggle for independence and for a long time thereafter; and boundary commissions, such as that of Felix de Azara in the Plata region, were promoting both scientific and historical studies.

In Spain, that zeal for historical writing which Becker has described as one of the stigmata of the Enlightenment led to the promising enterprise of Juan Bautista Muñoz, whom the court commissioned to write a new history of the New World; a Spanish translation of Adam Smith's *Wealth of Nations* was published at Madrid and was dedicated to the King's Chief Minister; and the climax came in 1789 when the court sent out an ambitious politico-scientific mission, headed by Alejandro Malaspina, to gather data on which a thoroughgoing reform of the Spanish régime in America was to be based. Two of these enterprises afford interesting evidence of the continuity of the Enlightenment in Spain, for one of the most admirable representatives of its earlier stages, the now aged Antonio de Ulloa, was consulted by both Muñoz and Malaspina, and the latter described himself as Ulloa's protégé.

Malaspina's mission is especially noteworthy because it shows first, how in these closing years of the Englightenment political reform as well as humanitarianism and the promotion of useful knowledge became an avowed purpose of the leaders of that movement in Spain; and second, how Italy as well

[ 17 ]

as France, England, and Germany stimulated that movement in the Iberian world. Though Malaspina served the Spanish crown continuously from an early age, he was Italian born and he never learned to speak Spanish without a foreign accent; and when, about 1795, after his return from his expedition to America, he proposed radical reforms in the government of the Spanish Empire, one of his critics stressed this Italian element in Malaspina's mental make-up, saying: "Whoever has attentively observed modern Italy either by direct contact with its people or through reading its historians, will have to agree that one of the clearest traces of the world dominion which the Italians once enjoyed is their invincible propensity for discussing the policy and government that other nations—the great powers of the present age—ought to adopt. Even in their present weakened condition, the Italians still discuss these questions with a zeal that could hardly have been exceeded by the august Roman Senate in the days of Mark Antony, Pompey, and Caesar, when Rome was actually lord of the universe. Malaspina is completely dominated by this political itch of his fellow countrymen, the violence of which has been greatly increased by the Italian books that he has read . . . and perhaps he is also obsessed by a desire to gain the kind of notoriety that Abbé Raynal has enjoyed."

This passage expresses the spirit of the hostile forces that were rising up against the Enlightenment in the Spanish Empire just as the movement was reaching its climax. If, as many authorities believe, the Philosophers unconsciously helped to bring on the French Revolution, they thereby contributed to the defeat of many of the conscious purposes of their activity throughout the eighteenth century. This is illustrated by the experience of the Spanish Empire, where, as in England and elsewhere, the French Revolution provoked a reaction against much that was best in the Enlightenment. The reaction was typified by the fate of Muñoz's history and Malaspina's expedition. The first volume of Muñoz's *Historia del Nuevo Mundo* was published in 1793; but the work was then suspended and it was never resumed. In 1795 Malaspina was disgraced and imprisoned, the reports of his politico-scientific expedition were scattered and many of them destroyed, and the court abandoned all serious thought of reform in America.

The ferment that the court itself had encouraged could not be stopped, and, as it proved, the alternative to reform was revolution. In Spanish America as in other parts of the world, revolution tended to defeat some of the main purposes of the Enlightenment, and yet in the end enough of it remained to alter profoundly both of the rôles that Latin

America had played in relation to that movement. In its passive rôle, thanks to the writings of Humboldt and other like-minded interpreters, the newly independent Latin America, though still retaining its predominantly Iberian character, was viewed with a sympathy in the rest of the European world of the nineteenth century that had never been extended to it in the eighteenth century. In its active rôle, the new Latin America inherited some of the zeal for reform, humanitarianism, and useful knowledge that had animated the eighteenth-century philosophers; and this remnant constituted the core of the Latin American liberalism of the nineteenth century.

## BIBLIOGRAPHICAL NOTE

Most of the important works dealing with the rôle of Latin America in the Enlightenment are cited in connection with other essays in this volume. See especially Mr. Marchant's article for works on Portugal and Brazil. Only a few works, of special significance for some of the topics discussed in this essay, are listed below.

For the background of the Enlightenment in Spain see: G. Delpy, *L'Espagne et l'esprit européen: l'œuvre de Feijóo (1725–1760)* (Paris, 1936). A critical account of the subject is contained in Marcelino Menéndez y Pelayo's classic *Historia de los heterodoxos españoles,* vol. III (Madrid, 1881). Scientific and political aspects of it are discussed in Pedro de Novo y Colson, ed., *Viaje político-científico alrededor del mundo por las corbetas Descubierta y Activa al mando de los capitanes de Navío D. Alejandro de Malaspina y D. José de Bustamante y Guerra desde 1789 à 1794* (Madrid, 1885); Hector R. Ratto, *Alejandro Malaspina: Viaje al Río de la Plata en el siglo XVIII* (Buenos Aires, 1938); Marius André, "Le Baron de Nordenflicht . . . et les mineurs allemands au Pérou," *Revue de l'Amérique latine,* VIII (1924), 289–306; Arturo Arnaiz y Freg, "Don Fausto de Elhuyar y de Zubice," *Revista de historia de América,* No. 6 (1939), pp.75–96; and Arthur P. Whitaker, *The Huancavelica Mercury Mine* (Cambridge, Mass., 1941). Some of the foregoing bring out the rather neglected contribution of Germany to the Enlightenment in Latin America. For Goethe, see Walter Wadepuhl, *Goethe's Interest in the New World* (Jena, 1934). An interesting example of recent criticism of the Enlightenment in Latin America is contained in F. A. Encina, "Gestación de la independencia," *Revista chilena de historia y geografía,* vol. 89, no. 97 (1940), especially §8, pp.33 ff., and §13, pp. 53–54.

# TRACES OF FRENCH ENLIGHTEN-
# MENT IN COLONIAL HISPANIC
# AMERICA [1]

*By* ROLAND D. HUSSEY

"FRENCH ENLIGHTENMENT" means, in this paper, ideas developed in France, based upon the rejection of classical authority, upon insistence on the need for experimental investigation, and upon acceptance of the conclusions of such experimentation even when they conflicted with earlier cherished beliefs.

A basis for the Enlightenment was laid in the works of such Frenchmen as Bodin, Montaigne, Descartes, and Gassendi, and Jansenism, though theologically "fundamentalist," contributed much to the breakdown of Aristotelian authority. But the real Enlightenment had English sources. It was to some degree the child of Bacon and Newton, but was based especially on the "sensationalism" of the philosophers, Hobbes and Locke, and the later rationalist, Hume. The Germans Leibnitz and Christian Wolf, though less important to France than were the English, also had an influence. Baldly stated, "sensationalism" meant an insistence that only the evidence of the senses had validity in a search for truth. These ideas, first powerfully advocated in France by Voltaire, were taken up and developed by a generation of thinkers, in all fields but especially in the social sciences. They lead ultimately to "revolutionary philosophy." The so-called *Encyclopédistes* and the French branch of Freemasonry were especially active in popularization and dissemination of the political aspects.

The Enlightenment was widely current in the Iberian peninsula.[2] Such Jansenist works in translation as Arnauld's *Arte de pensar* (1759) and Jacquier's *Instituciones filosóficas* (1787) were a main road to knowledge of Descartes. The sensationalist philosopher, Verney, was as well known in Spain as in his native Portugal. The Portuguese Almeida and the Spanish Feijóo, religiously orthodox but philosophically eclectic, greatly popularized, in their respective lands, the ideas of Bacon, Newton, Bayle, and the *Encyclopédistes*. The Spanish Jesuit Antonio Eximeno was an enthusiast for Locke and Condillac. The Peruvian born Olavide and the Francophile Aranda, both of them Masons, were typical of a host of enlightened men in Spanish office.

Private opposition to the new ideas, like Feijóo's refutation (1752) of Rousseau's *Discours* (1750), drew attention to the books at least as effectively as it combated them. The Spanish government offered less opposition than might be supposed, though it proscribed violently heretical or revolutionary writings, and its policy grew more rigid at the time of the French Revolution. The "Index" of 1790 prohibited the works, or the important part of the works, of Bayle, Bossuet, Brisson, Brissot de Warville, Burlamaqui, Diderot, the *Encyclopédie,* Helvetius, Holbach, La Fontaine, Marmontel, Montaigne, Montesquieu, Raynal, Rousseau, and Voltaire. It laid restrictions upon Bodin, Bayle, Condillac, Jansen, and Moreri's *Dictionnaire.* The supplement to the "Index" (1805) added more of Condillac, some of Condorcet, Necker, and Filangieri, a French version of Locke's *Essay concerning human understanding,* and the works of Mably and Volney. But most of the decrees appeared after the named works had long been in circulation, and were only slightly effective.

The works of Buffon, Descartes, Duhamel, Forbonnais, Gassendi, Hobbes, Hume, Jacquier, Lamarck, Lavoisier, Leibnitz, Malebranche, Newton, Nollet, Pascal, Quesnay, Sigaud, Saverien, Turgot, Verney, and Wolf were apparently never proscribed. One or more of those of Bossuet, Brisson, Buffon, Condillac, Filangieri, Hume,

Jacquier, La Fontaine, Locke, Marmontel, Montaigne, Pascal, Verney, and Voltaire were published with Spanish imprints. Some of the imprints may have been false. Even if so, like the Spanish versions of Rousseau published in London or "Charleston," they would not have been published in Spanish, anywhere, unless assured of a Spanish market. Raynal's *Histoire philosophique* was published in a satisfactory Spanish version by the Duke of Almodóvar under the pseudonym of Malo de Luque (Madrid, 1784–1790) and at least eleven volumes of an acceptable version of the *Encyclopédie* came out as the *Enciclopedia metódica, dispuesta por orden de materias* (Madrid, 1788-1794).

Enlightened doctrines became the norm in Spain. The universities, including finally that of Salamanca, modernized their curricula, 1769–1787; the General of the Spanish Barefoot Carmelites advised his startled convocation (1781) to read modern philosophy including Bacon, Locke, Gassendi, Descartes, Newton, and Condillac; Father Manuel Maria Truxillo, Commissary General of the Franciscans, said much the same thing in his *Exhortación pastoral* (Madrid, 1786); the Inquisitors themselves became "about as much Jansenists, or better said, Voltairists, as the suspects." The highly "enlightened" library that Miranda owned in Madrid suggests the possibilities along that line.

Freemasonry flourished among the influential classes, shifting from English to French type with the formation of the *Grande Oriente Nacional de España* (1780) under Aranda as Grand Master.

Portuguese contacts were more with England than with France, and modernization was less outstanding than in Spain, but changes in the same direction were under way. Even before the work of Verney, unsuccessful efforts to modernize instruction at the University of Coimbra showed an acquaintance with the writings of men like Bacon and Newton, and the Crown created various academies. Notable advances occurred from 1750 to 1777, during the domination of Pombal. That minister's *Arcadia de Lisboa,* established in 1757, had the chief function of fostering the Enlightenment. The new doctrines spread widely, especially in the natural sciences, and entered the University through the statute of 1772. Freemasonry, which had reached Portugal in 1733, became common in the army and upper class. Though both the new ideas and Freemasonry were persecuted during the severe reaction that followed the fall of Pombal, they were not eradicated from the national life. The *Arcadia* was allowed to disappear, but was well replaced by the *Academia real das sciencias* (1779) and Freemasonry remained strong enough to achieve a national Grand Lodge in 1804.

II

Ideas so widely spread in Europe reached Latin America by many channels. The well organized book-trade plentifully supplied works permitted by the authorities. The cargoes of two ships that reached Callao from Spain in 1785 included 35,320 volumes of Spanish works, and 2392 of foreign. There is no indication of the nature of any of these, but about one thousand volumes shipped to the rather backward Philippines ten years later, though mostly standard Spanish or Latin tomes, included science by Duhamel, a copy of Moreri's *Diction-naire,* and six copies of the *Neptune Oriental.*[3]

Officials, merchants, emigrants, and scientists [4] went constantly from Spain or Portugal to America, and Americans as constantly visited the Peninsula, and often France and other parts of Europe. A type of enlightened Spaniard reached America in the exile there of the rebel Picornell and his companions, part of them Freemasons. Ideas were ineradicably carried in migrating heads, and scientific apparatus and books made part of many men's baggage to America. The libraries carried out by Archbishop Caballero y Góngora and Bishop Hernández Milanés were larger than most, but were examples of many others. The Mexican Enderica

[ 28 ]

commissioned traveling friends to bring back books from New Orleans, among other places. José Antonio Rojas while in Europe gathered scientific apparatus and books from as far as St. Petersburg, and in 1774 shipped ten special cases back to Chile, supposedly licensed by the Inquisition though they held "foreign books, uncommon . . . and some prohibited."

Few of the high officials of Church and State sent to America in the last half century were reactionary men, and so many of them revealed modernism, and insistence on experimental science in their comments on education, that they must have belonged entirely to the Enlightenment. Archbishop-viceroy Caballero y Góngora in Bogotá remarked (1789), in regard to the new university there, "all the object of the plan should be directed to substituting the useful exact sciences for those merely speculative, in which up to now time has most regrettably been lost." Viceroy Revilla Gigedo advised his successor in Mexico (1794) that "much reform is needed . . . in the method of studies [in the university]. . . . There is no *gabinete,* nor collection of *máquinas* for studying modern experimental physical sciences; the library has few good works, especially modern ones." Such comments were typical. Viceroy Guirior even brought books to Mutis (1773) as a gift from Linnæus.[5]

[ 29 ]

Lack of a university in Brazil caused a large proportion of the intellectuals of that colony to attend Coimbra, often with further study at Montpellier and sometimes elsewhere in France.[6] Spanish Americans who studied or traveled in Europe vary all the way from obscure scholars to later leaders for independence. The Mexican Beristain, who at the University of Valencia (1778) publicly defended the philosophy of Verney and Jacquier; apostles of modernism like Baquíjano, Díaz de Gamarra and Goicoechea; and the patriot leaders Belgrano and O'Higgins, are a few of the multitude influenced by life in the Old World. So many Cuban youths studied with the refugee French Sulpicians at Baltimore that in 1803 Spain sent a ship to bring them back to avoid ideological contamination.[7]

Contact with foreigners within the colonies was also strong. Contrabandists were nearly everywhere at all times, and had a semi-legal status during periods when adequate trade with Spain was cut by war. No less than 175 French ships traded in Chile and Peru from 1695 to 1751, and they were probably as numerous in many years in the Plata and parts of the Caribbean. During the war of 1779–1783, trade with or via France and the French Antilles was common. French ships were admitted to American ports, even though reluctantly, during the Republican era. Many cases are recorded in which contrabandists sold books to colonials, from the Frenchman who furnished a Bible and seven other books to a Chilean priest in 1700 to the Dutchman who supplied the demand for French revolutionary literature in New Spain and Venezuela about 1797.[8] Around-the-world voyages and the visits of French scientific missions throughout the century brought Americans into contact with men like Frezier, Bougainville, Feuillé, La Condamine, Jussieu, Chappe d'Auteroche, and Bonpland. Scientists like Loefling, Jacquin, or Humboldt, and foreign experts sent by the Spanish Crown, including the naturalist Haënke and such mining technicians as Nordenflycht and Helm, were just as truly agents of French Enlightenment though from other countries.

The Franco-Spanish alliance against England facilitated a stay of several weeks in Caracas (1782) by the whole complement of officers of the Comte de Segur's French warship. Men from Cumana were serving in English or French ships for lack of other employment, in 1805. The British political exile Thomas Muir, while visiting Governor Borica in California on his flight from Australia (1796), delighted the governor with first-hand tales of the French Revolution, giving, as the governor wrote, "very circumstantial accounts of all that occurred," and painting "in vivid colors the characters of the principal personages." [9]

The proximity, and the later annexation, of French Louisiana, gave special emphasis to the foreign problem in New Spain, and hospitality to the unfortunate permitted refugees from the revolutionary French West Indies to enter Cuba, Venezuela, and Mexico. The Venezuelans included a number who claimed to have fled religious persecution by the English masters of Grenada, Tobago, and Trinidad. The introduction of regular troops in the 1760's brought in many French professional soldiers. The Anglo-Spanish war of 1779–1783 reinforced them. The legal status of the French Republican agents to Venezuela, Roume [10] and De Pons, is not clear, but at least they were there. Many of the French residents scattered throughout Spanish America seem to have settled down, however they arrived, as physicians. Others were cooks or hairdressers.

French contacts in Brazil were distinctly fewer, but voyagers and traders did find their way there. As examples, note the case of the impious French poet de Parny, at Rio de Janeiro in 1773, and the seaman Landolphe in 1800, or the men met by Lindley in 1802. Incidentally, Muir stopped for a visit on his way to Australia, and had sufficiently close relations with some friars to present them an inscribed book.

Many of these French contacts inseminated Hispanic Americans with the Enlightenment. Once sown, it spread widely among Americans who had never been in Europe and perhaps had never seen a Frenchman. The Peruvian Peralta and the Mexican Alzate never left their native lands, but they corresponded with members of the Academy of Sciences in Paris after contacts with French visitors. The private press of Nariño has received more than its due; its value was insignificant compared to the spread of ideas through the Spanish American periodicals, or through discussions in cafés and literary associations, or through borrowed books. The Inquisition records frequently mention the latter. Enderica in Mexico borrowed two of Rousseau's works and part of the *Encyclopédie* from the seaman Maurelle. Rojas' copies of Bayle, Holbach, Montesquieu, and others circulated in Chile, and Nordenflycht lent Voltaire's *Henriàde,* Montesquieu's *Esprit des lois,* and other works to persons in Peru. One can only speculate on how many other cases escaped detection, as he reads that in 1768 the receiver of the tribunal of the Inquisition in Mexico sold books seized from others as prohibited, and that the Argentine Maciel, as

Comisario of the Inquisition in Buenos Aires, read the works which he seized from others.

### III

Traces of the French Enlightenment are found in every book that deals at first hand, or through modern research from first-hand sources, with the intellectual status of Hispanic America in the latter part of the eighteenth century or with the history of Freemasonry. The *"leyenda negra,"* that Spain deliberately hampered colonial scholarly activities, has been under attack for some forty years. The most persistent calumny of all, the phrase attributed to Charles IV, "it is not fitting to have Enlightenment *(ilustración)* generally in America," was long ago demolished.

Without attempting, therefore, again to prove the general fact of the existence of new institutions and ideas and modernization of old, one can seek pertinent details in the lives of scholars, the history of schools, the contemporary publications, the inventories of libraries, and the history of Freemasonry. All prove a conclusion that could be guessed from the better-known observations of travelers, or the history of repressive measures by Church or State, or that of conspiracies and revolts:

in the last fifty years of the colonial era a reading knowledge of French and use of French books was common in the better class, and French ideas and ideals were warmly advocated or admired by many who knew them only through intermediaries.

The above was partly true even before 1750.[11] Before 1681, in fact, Sigüenza in Mexico was familiar with Gassendi and explained the Cartesian vortices along with the Copernican system.

Peralta, probably affected by the irruption of French traders into the Pacific, wrote a French poem by 1703, translated a play of Corneille a few years later, corresponded with Feijóo, and left a library probably depleted by poverty but packed with French and prohibited works. A recent writer calls him *"el primer afrancesado."* The textbook of Salgado, *Cursus medicus mexicanus . . . Pars prima physiologica* (Mexico, 1727) made only a faint-hearted start at teaching the new doctrines promised by its full title, but it reflected the growth of modern speculation and was the first book on physiology published anywhere in the New World. Feijóo was widely read; Descartes and Newton and Leibnitz were perhaps taught in Quito by 1736, chiefly by Jesuits; and Muriel in the Plata advanced some modern ideas by 1749. Llano Zapata, in an account of the Lima earthquake published in Madrid in 1748, cited Boyle, Gassendi, Duhamel,

Godin, and the *Memoires* of the French Academy of Sciences.

In the next quarter century, the outstanding occurrence was an attack on Aristotle. Llano Zapata, who started the campaign (1758) while in Spain, was later back in Peru. Other men there, in Venezuela, and in Buenos Aires fought the same fight, 1770–1771. Jesuits like Clavigero in Mexico, and Aldunate in Cordoba, seem to have introduced some novelties before 1767, and Juan Chacón proposed a chair of Physics for Habana in 1761 and taught the subject in the Seminary there in 1774. As men like Mutis and Moreno y Escandón in Bogotá, Goicoechea in Guatemala, Maciel in Buenos Aires, Llano Zapata and Luna y Pizarro in Peru, Aguirre in Ecuador, and Alzate in Mexico went to work, Descartes, Gassendi, Newton, and Leibnitz rose steadily in acceptance, at least as part of eclecticism. Coriche's *Oración vindicativo del honor de las letras* (Puebla, 1763) advertised Rousseau to Hispanic America by lengthily attacking one of his works. The textbooks of Díaz de Gamarra printed in Mexico in 1774, *Elementa recentioris philosophiae* and *Academias filosóficas* evidently had "sensationalist" content that foreshadowed the apparent reflection of Locke in Gamarra's *Errores del entendimiento humano* (Puebla, 1781).

Inventories of two libraries show significant collections.[12] Manuel Maria de la Torre, an official who died at Puerto Cabello in 1763, kept a locked chest with some thirty-four volumes. At least twelve were French, including a bilingual dictionary, the *Esprit des lois,* works of Molière and La Fontaine, and a "modern logic, or art of speaking the truth." Jean Baptiste Prevost of New Orleans, dying in 1769, left some three hundred volumes, naturally mostly in French. They included Locke and Robertson in that language, Montaigne, Bayle, Montesquieu's *Lettres persanes* and *Esprit des lois,* the works of Rousseau and Voltaire, a *Secrets des Flamagons* [i. e., *Francmasons*], and what probably were the works of Leibnitz and Wolf. Individual Freemasons appeared in Mexico, Peru, and Cuba in the period, but the only known lodge, that of Havana, was established (1762) by a British regiment and presumably disappeared with the regiment.

The flowering of all that had gone before occurred after 1775. Many of the scholars already named lived on, and were joined by a galaxy of now famous teachers and editors: Rodríguez de Mendoza, Baquíjano and Unánue in Lima, Mutis, Caldas and Socorro Rodríguez in Bogotá, Espejo in Quito, Terrazas in Chuquisaca, Salas in Santiago, Montero and Chorroarín in Buenos Aires, Marrero

[ 37 ]

in Caracas, Caballero in Havana, and Jácobo Villaurrutía in Guatemala and Mexico. Around them clustered satellites hardly less brilliant; from their classrooms came the famous generation that won their nation's independence; from their pens came short-lived but influential periodicals. Teachers, pupils, and periodicals were almost synonymous with the liberal *Sociedades económicas de amigos de la patria* that sprang up so widely in the last years of the colonial régime.

The writings and teachings of these men were conspicuous for the citation of French enlightened philosophers and scientists. Baquíjano, in his *Elogio . . . de Jáuregui* (Lima, 1781) mentioned among others Montesquieu, Linguet, and Raynal. Alzate, in his *Observaciones sobre la física, historia natural, y artes útiles* (Mexico, 1787) mentions among others the scientists Reaumur, Nollet, Monnet, and the *Encyclopédie*. The last, he said, was an *"obra bien conocida"* and the outcome of *"los mayores esfuerzos á que puede elevarse el genio,"* though he disapproved its attacks on religion. His *Gazeta de literatura* (Mexico, 1788–1795) shows similar mental traits, including attacks on Aristotelianism. The editors of the *Mercurio Peruano* (Lima, 1791–1795) on just one page managed to cite Reaumur, Duhamel, Newton, and Leibnitz, on another one Raynal and Montesquieu. They frequently used Bayle. They show familiarity with almost any other book that might be pertinent to this article, from the *Encyclopédie* to the writings of Hume and Lamarck. The men behind the *Gazeta de Guatemala* (1797–1810) dealt familiarly with Buffon, Condillac, Descartes, Pascal, Newton, Lalande, Lametrie, Laplace, Mesmer, and Quesnay. The *Papel periódico de Bogotá* (1791–1797) and the *Papel periódico de Habana* (1790–1804) were of the same type as their counterparts in other cities.

Students' theses at the University of Guatemala flatly advocated an eclectic philosophy in 1791 and 1802, and Father Matías de Córdova in his prize-winning essay (1796) for the Real sociedad patriótica de Guatemala, *Utilidades de que todos los Indios y Ladinos se vistan y calcen á la española* (Guatemala: Ignacio Beteta, 1798) cited Buffon and showed other traces of French ideas. Long before 1808 students at the University of Caracas heard openly of Bacon, Condillac, Brisson, Buffon, Descartes, Lamarck, Locke, and Newton. Between 1804 and 1807 they used as texts the logics of Verney and Condillac, the chemistry of Lavoisier, and works by Brisson, Sigaud, and Nollet.

In Cuba, Caballero proposed modern reforms in the University (1795), cited "Fasendo"—presumably Gassendi, at second hand—and Descartes in 1797, and explained such novel terms as *"métre"* to the puzzled readers of the *Papel periódico*. The influence of Condillac, Locke, and Pestalozzi—follower of Rousseau—is visible in plans of the *Sociedad patriótica* of Havana in 1808.[13] A Chilean *Discurso* (Santiago, c. 1801), probably by Salas, mentions casually or with some comment the works of foreign scientists including Gassendi, Descartes, Pascal, Bacon, Newton, Leibnitz, Locke, Malebranche, and Pauw. Another item[14] was an incomplete translation of Savarien's *Historia de las ciencias naturales* (Bogotá, 1791), and many works inspired—though unfavorably—by the French Revolution.

Clearly, in this later period knowledge of the works of the founders of the Enlightenment had been supplemented by those of the developers, especially Condillac and the natural scientists. There is also a perceptible trace of physiocracy in the American writings. Libraries of the period not only had books on those fields, but their contents suggest the sources of the knowledge of Rousseau and other social scientists which the political leaders showed after 1810. Partial information exists, for instance, on many libraries of the Plata, including those of Maciel (1788) and Bishop Azamos y Ramírez (1796); of Bishops Torrijos (c. 1794) and Hernández Milanés (c. 1803) of Mérida, Venezuela; of Quito in general (c. 1801); of the Colegio de San

Carlos in Lima (c. 1806); and of the Biblioteca Palafoxiana of the seminary in Puebla about the end of the colonial period.[15] That of Torrijos was evidently strong on modern works, at least in the sciences. Maciel and Azamos had Bayle, Voltaire, Rousseau, Montesquieu, and Raynal. That of Milanés included at least the philosophies of Condillac and Eximeno, Buffon's *Histoire naturelle,* and a French dictionary. Caldas testified as to the excellence of libraries in Quito. "Hardly a private person lacks one," he wrote, "and books that one cannot see in Bogotá I have found here." He mentioned using even recent issues of the *Mémoires* of the French Academy of Sciences, and works of Buffon, Maupertuis, Cassini, and Reaumur. The present holdings of the Biblioteca Palafoxiana, which probably added very few books after 1810, include large numbers of eighteenth-century books in French, including the works of Voltaire, Hume and Robertson. Descartes is present in a seventeenth-century edition. The traveler Stevenson stated that the library of San Carlos had many prohibited books.

Contemporary inventories [16] exist for the large collections of Viceroy-Archbishop Caballero y Góngora (c. 1783) and Nariño (1794), both in Bogotá, of Miranda's great collection of English books while at Havana (1783), of the large library

of the official Francisco de Ortega in Buenos Aires
(1790), and of the smaller lot left at the death of
Governor-General Gayoso de Lemos of Louisiana
in 1799. Caballero owned a scholarly collection of
about four hundred titles in two thousand volumes.
Among much other science, there occurs Newton's
*Principia.* Some four hundred volumes were in
French, including Hume, Locke, and Montesquieu's *Esprit des lois.* Over one third of the fifteen
hundred volumes of Nariño's library were in
French. In addition to Buffon, De la Fond, Necker,
and Descartes, these included the *Encyclopédie,*
works by Raynal, Montesquieu, and Voltaire, and
several treatises on the United States. Nothing by
Rousseau or Locke appears. Among the many
French or English works owned by Gayoso de
Lemos, only Buffon and six volumes on the French
Revolution are pertinent, but Ortega owned prac-
tically all the important works of the Enlightenment including Almeida, Bacon, and Newton.
Miranda's English library had Enlightened works.
Presumably Miranda's books were soon removed
from the country. Torrijos, Milanés, and Caballero
left their libraries for semi-public establishments.
Inventories for Lima (1813) and Guatemala
(1821) of books confiscated by the Inquisition over
many years show that many copies of all the most
"dangerous" political writings reached those coun-

tries, though they prove nothing about who had read them there before 1808.

French Freemasons were before the Inquisition in Mexico from 1785 and perhaps established lodges in Buenos Aires (1795) and in Cuba about that time. But an English lodge in Buenos Aires (1801) also has claims to be the first in that city; the first in Mexico (1806) was of the Scottish Rite; and if Miranda's mysterious *Gran Logia* existed at all, its headquarters were in London. The part of Freemasonry in introducing French Enlightenment into Spanish America cannot be proved large.[17]

IV

The intellectual life of Brazil was less developed than that of Spanish America. But it is easy to exaggerate the lack of intellectual development at any time, and conditions improved in the later part of the eighteenth century.[18] Traces of French Enlightenment, though fewer, are found. Such aspects of the general improvement as the creation of many "Academies" in Brazil from 1724, and the establishment of a *Gabinete de estudos de historia natural* in Rio (1784) and chairs of advanced mathematics in Pernambuco (1799), are strictly typical of the Enlightenment. The presence of many men in Brazil who had studied at Montpellier, and of a few like Manoel Ferreira de Camara Bittencourt é Sa, who had been in Paris and elsewhere in Europe, would justify the assumption of an influence. It can be proved chiefly in the existence of a French, or "Arcadian," school of literature, in records of conspiracies, and in the notable activities of secret societies.

The secret societies, supposedly for literary purposes, were numerous. They often had a political tinge, and some were almost certainly Masonic. There were ten Masonic lodges in Montpellier when that city was frequented by Brazilian students, aside from those in Portugal. Some writers believe that there were Masons in Rio in the mid-eighteenth century, and that they backed the Mineiro conspiracy of 1789. Neither statement is well authenticated. But a lodge was set up in Bahia in 1797, possibly in connection with the visit of a French ship; Landolphe attended a Masonic meeting in Rio in 1800, with the Viceroy's son and many dignitaries of Church and State; the lodge "Reunião" was established under the Grand Orient of France in 1801; and Lindley met Masons in 1802.[19]

The conspiracy of Tiradentes in Minas Geraes (1789) was apparently fostered more by the example of the United States than by the abstractions of France, but it had some French inspiration.

After the French Revolution began, influences from France became stronger. The conspiracy at Rio (1794) brought out charges that the accused, at their Academy, "always talked of France and its rebellion with praise, always attacking religion," and that they spoke "with approval of the present regime in France." The conspiracy of Bahia (1798) had the avowed purpose of establishing a "democratic government" and shows plainly that French political ideas were growing.

Books are included in the inventories of goods sequestrated,[20] in connection with the conspiracy of 1789, from such suspects as Carlos Correia de Toledo e Mello, Luis Vieira da Silva, Claudio Manoel da Costa, Ignacio José de Alvarenga Peixoto, Colonel José de Rezende Costa, and Father Manoel Rodrigues da Costa. The last four had relatively small collections, but among them they owned products of Moreri, Bayle, Voltaire, Almeida, Burlamaqui, and Marmontel, as well as dictionaries and literary works of such men as Molière, Racine, and Boileau. Rodrigues da Costa had a three-volume Milton, probably in English. Correia de Toledo's general library of some two hundred volumes included sixty-one titles. Thirteen titles were in French and two in English. Along with French grammars, dictionaries, and religious items appear the works of Bayle, Montesquieu, and Verney. Vieira da Silva's approximately one thousand volumes were strong on modern law and science. The 249 titles included at least eighty-seven that plainly belong to the Enlightenment, most of them French. In addition to French and English dictionaries, one finds included Feijóo's *Teatro crítico,* Verney, Wolf, Descartes, Condillac, Burlamaqui, Vattel, Montesquieu, Duhamel, Mably, Marmontel, Robertson's *History of America* (in French), and incomplete sets of Voltaire and the *Encyclopédie.* Vieira da Silva also had several items borrowed from the Intendant, which included something by Mably and by Marmontel.

Lindley, who had little good to say of conditions around Bahia in 1802, was favorably impressed by the learning of Father Francisco Agustinho Gomes. The latter was wealthy and devoted to science. He read French and English and had in his large library the *Encyclopédie* and the works of Buffon and Lavoisier. According to testimony at the time of the Bahia conspiracy, he passed on news from French and English newspapers. Inventories at that time of two lesser libraries of his city show an astonishing proportion of French. The seventy-four volumes owned by Cipriano José Barata de Almeida included thirty-one titles. Eighteen were French, and most of the others represented modern science. The works of Condillac, the chemistry of "Fourer," and possibly the chemistry of Lavoisier and the natural history of Buffon can be identified. There is also a history in French of the United States. The twenty-eight volumes owned by *tenente* Hermogenes Francisco de Aguilar of the 2nd regiment showed twenty-two titles. Only eight were French, but these included Voltaire's *Dictionnaire philosophique* and Bayle's *Dictionnaire historique*. There were also a French *Vocabulaire* and two Portuguese aids to learning French. Since all these libraries—unlike most of the Spanish American ones discussed—are known because their owners were regarded as dangerous, they may not be typical. But it is most improbable that the possessors had a monopoly of French books in Brazil, or refused to lend them to their friends! [21]

V

Properly to evaluate these traces, one would need careful studies of every region and subject and of the groups that combated or rejected the Enlightenment, and comparable studies of English and United States influences. Facts known from the sources used upon the French, in this paper, make it safe to say that French influences were nearly everywhere greater than those of other foreign nations. Those of Anglic origin were strong in Mexico,

Chile, and the Plata, and may have outweighed the French in Brazil and Cuba. The Antilles including Cuba, and Central America aside from Guatemala, apparently felt little of any new stimulus before 1808. Provinces generally were less affected than the major cities. But there can be no doubt of the widespread nature of the traces.

The Enlightenment clearly influenced many men in the eighteenth century, and the whole of the generation that came to maturity about 1808 and led the struggle for independence. A recent authority regards Rousseau's *Social Contract,* Quesnay's *General maxims of political economy,* and Condillac's *Treatise on the sensations* as the "ideological sources of the revolution" in the Argentine.[22] The statement would hold true elsewhere. One might need to add Locke as to Venezuela, and it is unwise to forget the religious effect of Bayle, Voltaire, and the *Encyclopédie,* or the practical effect of French and United States political instruments and manifestos. But the basic importance of "sensationalism" applied by the French to human institutions is well agreed to.

One notes how universally the French works most owned or cited were in skeptical philosophy, or the social or natural sciences. The Hispanic peoples had adequate belles-lettres of their own; consciously or not they were filling in from French sources the gaps left by Hispanic thought in their preparation for mental as well as political independence. The enthusiasm of Humboldt as he surveyed the intellectual status of America from Mexico and Havana to Caracas and Quito [23] seems less strange to one who has looked at colonial writings than to writers who have looked only at nineteenth-century propaganda. The proportion of French Enlightenment in the total mental make-up of colonial Hispanic Americans was no doubt infinitesimal, but it was large among the groups where it most could count.

[1] Normally, statements are backed by citations only in case experts in the field might be unable to locate their source.

[2] Cf.: M. Méndez Bejarano, *Historia de la filosofía en España* (Madrid, [c. 1926]), 335–383; M. Menéndez y Pelayo, *Historia de los heterodoxos españoles* (Madrid, 1911–     ), v. 6; N. Díaz y Pérez, *Franc-masonería española* (Madrid, 1894), 139–144, 164–167, 179–186; J. Sempere y Guarinos, *Ensayo de una bibliotheca española* (Madrid, 1785–1789), IV, 207–251; F. Miranda, *Archivo,* VII (Caracas, 1930), 144–151; F. de Almeida, *Historia de Portugal* (Coimbra, 1922–1929), V, 225–231, 409–440; E. Borges Graïnha, *Histoire de la franc-maçonnerie en Portugal* (Lisbonne, 1913), 31–63; T. Braga, *Historia da universidade de Coimbra* (Lisboa, 1892–1902), II, *passim;* J. Mendes dos Remedios, *Historia da literatura portuguesa* (Coimbra, 1930), 381–431.

[3] *Estado que manifiesta los efectos*—A.G.I., Ind. Gen. 2428.

[4] Cf.: F. de Figueiredo, "Do aspecto scientifico na coloniçacão Portuguesa da America," *Revista de historia,* XIV (Lisboa, 1925), 189–220.

[5] E. Posada (ed.), *Relaciones del mando* (Bogotá, 1910), 252; Revilla Gigedo, *Instrucción reservada* (Mexico, 1831), 10; J. E. Smith (ed.), *Selection of the correspondence of Linnaeus* (London, 1821), 525.

[6] Cf.: J. M. Pereira da Silva, *Os varões illustres do Brasil* (2 v., Paris, 1858); A. Motta, *Historia da litteratura brasileira* (2 v., São Paulo, 1930).

[7] Study in the United States continued for years: C. M. Trelles, "Sobre la prohibición . . . ," *Bol. del Archivo Nac.* XXXIII (Havana, 1934),

20–25; Tacón to Secretary González Salmon, Philadelphia, 3 and 13 May, 1828—A.H.N., Est. 5654.

[8] "Informe del virey Aviles (1801)," *Revista de la Biblioteca Publica de Buenos Aires,* III (Buenos Aires, 1881), 474–477; anonymous contemporary account—B.N. (Paris), MSS. Franç. Nouv. Acq. 2610, fol. 48; Carbonell to Godoy, Caracas, 23 March 1798—A.G.I., Est. 70; *Estado general de las embarcaciones*—Mata Linares MSS (Acad. de la historia, Madrid), v. 68.

[9] Cagigal á S. M., Cumaná, 29 July 1805—Mata Linares MSS, v. 68; M. Masson, "Odyssey of Thomas Muir," *Amer. Hist. Rev.* XIX (October, 1923), 49–72.

[10] For Roume, ca. 1797–1798, see papers in Archivo Nacional (Caracas), *Gual y España,* t. 1, no. 23.

[11] *Belerofonte matemática,* and *Libra astronomica.* The second was printed in Mexico, 1690, but written in 1681, and it includes the first.

[12] R. de Basterra, *Una empresa del siglo XVIII* (Caracas, 1925), 140; "Inventory of the estate of . . . Prevost," *La. Hist. Quarterly* IX (July, 1926), 429–457.

[13] A. Bachiller y Morales, *Apuntes para la historia de las letras* (2d ed., Havana, 1936–1937), I, 304–307, 346–347; O. Morales y del Campo, "Evolución de las ideas pedagógicos en Cuba," *Revista Bimestre Cubana,* XXII (1927), 713–732; C. Trelles y Govín, *Bibliografía de la Universidad de la Habana* (Havana, 1938), *passim.*

[14] E. Posada, *Bibliografía bogotana* (Bogota, 1917), no. 62. Humboldt [*Essai politique* II (Paris, 1811), 18] says that a translation of Lavoisier's "Elements of chémistry" was printed in Mexico. It is not mentioned by standard bibliographies.

[15] J. M. Gutiérrez, *Orígen y desarrollo de la enseñada . . . en Buenos Aires* (Buenos Aires, 1915), 484–487; J. T. Medina, *Inquisición en el Rio de la Plata* (Santiago, 1899), 255; H. García Chuecos, *Estudios de historia colonial venezolana* (Caracas, 1937), 175–178, 201–203; I. J. Barrera, *Quito colonial* (Quito, 1922), 60–62; R. R. Caillet-Bois, *Ensayo sobre el Rio de la Plata y la revolución francesa* (Buenos Aires, 1929), 19–25.

[16] J. Torre Revello, "La biblioteca del virrey-arzobispo," *Boletín del Instituto de Investigaciones históricas,* IX (Buenos Aires, 1929), 27–45, and "Libros procedentes de expurgos . . . 1813," *ibid.,* XV (1932), 329–351; Caillet-Bois, *op. cit.,* iii–xiii; E. Posada, *El precursor* (Bogota, 1903), 164–191; F. Miranda, *Archivo,* VII (Caracas, 1930), 161–165; *Causa mortuaria . . . Gayoso de Lemos*—A.G.I., Papeles de Cuba, 169; M. Mérida, "Historia crítica de la inquisición de Guatemala," *Boletín del archivo general del gobierno,* III (Guatemala, 1937), 127–151.

[17] Cf.: C. A. Brockaway, "Masonería en Cuba," *Revista bimestre cubana*, XXXVII (Havana, 1936), 282–296; M. V. Lazacano, *Sociedades secretas . . . en Buenos Aires*, I (Buenos Aires, 1927), 40–92; B. Oviedo Martínez, "La logia lautarina," *Revista Chilena de historia e geografía*, LXII (Santiago, 1929), 105–126; A. R. Zuñiga, *La logia lautaro* (Buenos Aires, 1922), *passim*.

[18] Cf.: Motta, *op. cit.*, II, 231–469; Figueiredo, *op. cit.;* P. Moacyr, *A instrucção e o imperio* (São Paulo, 1936–1938), I, 9–38.

[19] J. Serrano, *Historia do Brasil* (Rio de Janeiro, 1931), 307; L. J. Dos Santos, *A inconfidencia Mineira* (São Paulo, 1927), 89–92; M. Behring (ed.), "A inconfidencia da Bahia em 1798," *Annaes da Bibliotheca nacional*, XLIII–XLIV (Rio de Janeiro, 1920–1921), iv–xl.

[20] *Autos da devassa. Inconfidencia Mineira* (Rio de Janeiro, 1936–1938), I, V, VI, *passim*, especially I, 397–402, 445–467.

[21] Behring, *op. cit.*, 186–187, 198–199.

[22] J. Ingenieros, *La evolución de las ideas argentinas* (Buenos Aires, 1937), I, 175–176.

[23] *Essai politique*, II (Paris, 1811), 9–24.

# SOME INTER-AMERICAN ASPECTS
# OF THE ENLIGHTENMENT

*By* Harry Bernstein

The Enlightenment in Spanish America, as in Europe, supplanted scholastic speculation by experimental investigation. The sweep of reasoned thought into America carried many ideas from Europe. British science, French philosophy, Spanish political reform made a considerable impression. The United States also shared in the intellectual expansion of the Enlightenment, and the New World adapted the concepts of Europe to American ways.

It was an age of freshly born inter-American interest, and cosmopolitan eighteenth-century life offered newer channels for transfer and exchange of thought between the Americas. The best thought of England, France, and Spain did not divert currents of American relations from recently established courses. Intellectual understanding with Spanish America was sought in colonial Boston, in the days of the Mathers. In form and purpose it was different from our contemporary interest, but in accordance with Puritan ideals it reflected hopes of spiritual unity of the Americas. The first Americans to seek the basis were Cotton Mather and Judge Samuel Sewall in New England.

Cotton Mather, an apostle of God's plans in America, studied Spanish so well that, in 1699, he published in Boston his *Religion Pura, to which is added La Fe del Christiano; En Veynte Quatro Articulos de la Institucion de Christo. An Essay to convey Religion into the Spanish Indies.* He was the first American to study Spanish in order to communicate with Hispanic America. In January, 1699, he confided to his Diary that "about this time understanding that the way for our communication with the *Spanish Indies* opens more and more, I sett myself to learn the *Spanish language.* . . . Accordingly I composed a little body of the *Protestant Religion* in certain articles, back'd with irresistible sentences of Scripture. This I turn'd into the Spanish tongue; and am now printing it with a Design to send it by all the ways that I can into the several parts of Spanish America. . . ."

Judge Samuel Sewall, friend of Mather, and prominent politically, gave definition to the design. A neighborly man, he wanted his American neighbors to think as he did. The Puritan world of "dreamers in Israel" required a capital, and Sewall yearned to see New Spain as the New Jerusalem of Puritan tradition. He also studied the language and its literature. Writing to the Secretary for Propagation of the Gospel in London, the Judge suggested "it would be well if you could set on foot the printing of the Spanish Bible in a fair Octavo, Ten Thousand Copies; and then you might attempt the bombing [sic] of Santa Domingo, the Havanna, Porto Rico, and Mexico itself. Mr. Leigh commends the Translation of the Cypriano Valera [Spanish dissenter] of which I am the Owner in Folio."

A period of European and American war against Spain furnished opportunity for Sewall's plan. When the Colombian, Carlos Sucre y Borda, ancestor of Bolivar's lieutenant, arrived in Boston in 1709, Sewall tried to convert him to the project. He loaned Sucre the copy of the Valera Bible, and learned what he could of Mexican life, people, and Aztec culture, asserting, "I rather think that Americana Mexicana will be the New Jerusalem."

Plans for spiritual approach bore no fruit. Puritan soil was too arid for newer forces emerging in the eighteenth century. Democracy, science, and learning were based upon man's progress in the New World, compared with European decline. A new identity of Americans, despite divergent origins, was suggested by the Chilean, Manuel de Salas. Son of the Age of Reason, political economist and writer, Salas perceived New World thought to be continental in type, different in its youth and strength from worn-out Europe which had contributed knowledge for so long. New World culture was no longer a dependent daughter of mother countries.

The forceful *criollismo* of the eminent Chilean protested against opinions, common then and now, "that we are inferior, that the writings of de Pauw and Sepúlveda make us unfit for science." Salas declared in 1801 that the task awaiting Spanish America was complete destruction of this imposture devised by European writers. Americans were vindicated, he wrote, by the works and just fame of Peralta, Franklin, and Molina. "Astronomy, electricity and history have taken on a new aspect in the hands of these famous Americans."

Benjamin Franklin effected a great stimulus upon Spanish American Enlightenment. Second to Newton in widespread popularity and influence, he mirrored the Age of Reason. He warmed the "climate of opinion" far more than did Thomas Jefferson, and appeared to Spanish Americans as the symbol of North American science and democracy. Franklin was the first American to attain membership in the Spanish Academy of History at Madrid. He became a Hispanist and his work was brought to Spanish America.

Salas in Chile, José Alzate y Ramirez in New Spain studied Franklin's scientific contributions. Dr. Alzate was a Mexican scientist who was well known in Europe. As editor of the *Gazeta de Literatura de Mexico,* he abetted Mexican acquaintance with Franklin, and Alexander Garden, the South Carolina botanist. Dr. Alzate told his subscribers that he "would need much paper to deal with the discoveries of Franklin," whose works he translated. He published in the *Gazeta* for 1790 some of Franklin's letters and papers on heat rays, optics, and waves.

A new intellectual link, forged from the effects of the Enlightenment, united scientists in America. The American Philosophical Society established exchange of transactions. Dr. Alzate read the work of Alexander Garden on cochineal and tobacco in the Transactions of that Society, which reached Mexico in 1790. The American Philosophical Society attained exchange relations with Academies in Seville, Madrid, and Valencia. It forwarded its Transactions to the "Academy at Mexico" in 1799. In 1801 the Society entrusted care of its periodic Spanish shipment to the enlightened Cuban, José de Arango, librarian of the *Sociedad Económica de Amigos del País de Habana.*

American historians such as John Pintard, Ebenezer Hazard, and Jeremy Belknap, founders of the oldest Historical Societies in Massachusetts and New York, corresponded on problems of Spanish American history and Indian civilization. They eagerly discussed the contents of Garcilaso de la Vega on the Inca, or Clavigero on the Aztec. Dr. Benjamin Smith Barton of the College of Philadelphia examined Spanish American sources dealing with Indian cultures. Barton was an eminent physician, whose influence was especially felt in Guatemala. There, his papers on the nature and incidence of goitre, published in Philadelphia in 1800, were extensively reviewed and cited in the *Gazeta de Guatemala,* beginning with the issue of 1801.

Barton's conclusion as to man's progress in the New World led him to clash with de Pauw, Buffon, and the historian William Robertson, but were similar to those of Manuel de Salas, for the reviewer concluded cryptically, "El Dr. Barton es criollo." The medical reputation of Drs. Barton, Rush, and Coxe of the Medical School at Philadelphia were sufficient for the *Gazeta de Guatemala* of 1802 to quote their opinions on the all-important discovery of vaccination.

Barton's theories were made known to Guatemalan enlightened circles by Dr. José Felipe Flores, a noted scientist himself and Honorary Physician to the Crown, although a *criollo*. The visits of Miranda and Bolívar have obscured the presence of Dr. Flores in this country in 1797. He had been authorized by the Crown to travel to perfect his studies, and came to Philadelphia to meet the leading figures in that center of science. A letter of his, dated 1797 and addressed to his Guatemalan colleague and teacher, Father Goicoechea, summarized for the Guatemalan public the achievements of the scientific world.

Another distinguished American scientist, Dr. Samuel Latham Mitchill, of Columbia College in New York, was not as well known in Spanish America at this time. But Mitchill was the first North American to reconcile scientific enlightenment and democracy by endorsing the Latin American struggle for liberation. Dr. Mitchill further set himself the task of illuminating the public on the accomplishments of Spanish American science. His address to the New York Historical Society in 1813 opened to American view the achievements of his Mexican, Colombian, and Peruvian colleagues.

Mitchill's sympathies did not prevent him from acknowledging the influence of Spain in the Spanish American Enlightenment. He discussed the contributions of writers from Oviedo to his contemporary, Azara. Describing the sums expended by Ruiz and Pavón in Peru, Drs. Sesse and Mociño in New Spain, Dr. Mutis and Caldas in Bogotá, Dr. Mitchill added, "I wish it was in my power to state the particulars for the improvement of American botany made by the Kings of Spain. There is not perhaps a government upon earth that has expended so much money for the advancement of this branch of natural history as that of the Castilian monarch."

Interest in Spanish America was beginning to appear in the United States. Histories of Inca and Aztec were read, and library collections were available. Newspapers were alert and attentive to agricultural discoveries in Chile in 1784—an event which stirred correspondence between Jeremy Belknap and Ebenezer Hazard. New York papers followed experiments in Peruvian bark or quinine conducted by the Madrid scientist, Dr. Casimiro Gómez Ortega.

Books dealing with Peru, Mexico, Venezuela, and Chile won markets for Boston, Salem, or New York publishers. Libraries in New York, Philadelphia, Newport, Boston, and other cities began to buy and receive books that educated interested readers to the Spanish and Portuguese half of the Americas. Popular magazines, published in different cities, serialized standard histories of Spanish and Portuguese settlement. A reading public found materials in the Harvard College Library, New York Society Library, New York Historical Society, Massachusetts Historical Society, Philadelphia Library Company, and the American Antiquarian Society.

Increased study of Spanish American antiquities

and history followed. Another result was the publication of Díaz del Castillo, Molina, Depons, and *La Araucana* within the United States. One can easily sense the pride of Dr. Mitchill when the edition of Molina was issued in 1808: "It is an honor to our age and country that the first translation into our own tongue should have been done at Middletown in Connecticut by one of our own literati and published in this city." The volume was dedicated to Dr. Benjamin Barton.

There were other ways in which streams of enlightenment were mingled in America. Knowledge of each region was supplied by that famous intermediary-scientist, Alexander von Humboldt, who was acquainted with scientific achievement in both continents. Francisco Caldas, student of Mutis and a journalist-astronomer reminiscent of the Mexican Alzate, reprinted in his *Seminario de la Nueva Granada,* the notices supplied by Humboldt on the studies of Jeremy Belknap, Manassah Cutler, and Dr. Barton. Caldas was led from this point to a desire to communicate with Americans: in 1811 the American Philosophical Society tersely recorded a request for relations, which "was sent by Pedro de la Lastra from Santa Fé de Bogotá. Also a Description of the Astronomical Observatory there, in charge of F. I. de Caldas, who seeks correspondence with Astronomers in the United States."

[ 61 ]

The American Philosophical Society, together with other societies, acquired scientific writings of Latin Americans. Interested individuals donated many contemporary scientific works such as that of Hipólito Ruiz, botanist of the Chile-Peru expedition of 1778, together with Dr. Hipólito Unánue's study of the coca plant. These additions engaged further attention, for in 1803, among books to be purchased, the American Philosophical Society ordered the "Mercurio Peruviano [sic] from its Commencement." Numerous works on Mexican antiquities and mineralogy were received, including "a box of minerals, 63 volumes and 4 numbers of the Journal de Physique [sic], accompanied by a letter continuing the subscription to the same as a donation to the Society," sent in 1807 by Juan Manuel de Ferrer of Vera Cruz. The Society kept in touch with the Spanish American mind in a period of growing international community.

Visits, articles, publication, collections, and indications of larger interest in Spanish America led to election of Spanish Americans to North American societies. After independence, such intellectuals as Silva Lisboa, José Bonifacio de Andrada e Silva, Dr. Gregorio Funes, Manuel Moreno, Pedro de la Llave, and Andrés del Río were chosen. Contributions were sometimes made, as when the American Philosophical Society published the Philadelphia lectures of the Mexican Dr. Del Río, on the Bequerel process.

The American Antiquarian Society followed these precedents. Its President, Isaiah Thomas, addressed the society in 1814 asking whether it should not be "one of our first endeavors to extend membership to gentlemen of distinguished characters in Spanish and Portuguese America, particularly the . . . former where it is believed many valuable antiquities of this continent may be procured." Article II of its earliest laws provided that "it shall be the duty of the Council to enquire concerning the character of persons living out of the Commonwealth proper to be elected honorary members, particularly in Spanish America." The society imitated the action of the American Philosophical Society, which as early as 1801 had nominated Dr. Alejandro Ramírez of the "junta of Guatemala." Ramírez, a figure of note in Cuba, Puerto Rico, and Central America, lived most of his life in Guatemala, Puerto Rico, and Cuba, where he died in 1821. His botanical discoveries and fellowship in the Royal Academy of History in Madrid justified the choice.

The Age of Reason was also accompanied by economic and political expansion of horizons. Contemporary concepts of the Noble Savage, and love for the primitive, symbolized the state of nature and the natural rights of man. Political philosophies, together with writings on the red man, expressed a sense of homogeneity in which North America was identified as the home of natural man, natural rights and sovereignty.

Madrid authorities attempted to exclude such thoughts from the colonies. Two works were banned: one, the Bible in Indian language, composed by John Eliot, prohibited in 1710; the other, a so-called Apocalypse of the supposed Iroquois chieftain, Chiokahaw, printed at Philadelphia in 1776. Newspapers, copies of the Declaration of Independence, the Constitution, pins, pendants, and other devices carried the democratic idea into the southern continent. Sometimes the idea of unity might be expressed in the religious language of Mather and Sewall, or it could be scientific, and finally political, as when Mariano Moreno in December of 1810 incorporated into the *Gaceta de Buenos Aires* Jefferson's defense of the future of Americans, as a young, virile people, written in his "Notes on Virginia."

Spanish American thought, already permeated by European ideas, began to seek in the past and future of the New World for the spirit of the age. North America reciprocated the new outlook. Additional methods were adopted after 1810. Diplomatic agents to Spanish America sought to spread understanding. Through the efforts of H. M. Brackenridge, American representative in Buenos Aires, the Argentine history of Dr. Funes was translated and printed in the United States. Part of the function of Jeremy Robinson in his diplomatic mission to Argentina, Chile, and Peru in 1818 was to invite correspondence between Dr. Samuel Latham Mitchill, Director of the New York Lyceum of Natural History, and noted Spanish Americans. Robinson visited Dr. Bonpland, the associate of Humboldt, Manuel de Salas, and Dr. Hipólito Unánue the Peruvian anatomist, conveying the message. Many gifts came to Dr. Mitchill from Bartolomé Muñoz, whose Cabinet of Natural History was the nucleus of the Buenos Aires Museum.

The generation that lived through the years of North and South American Independence, from 1783 to 1823, could see that relations between the two were developing in an era of war, and revolution. British and Napoleonic blockade had cut Latin America from European materials and markets. Practical problems were no less important to Spanish America than matters of rights, progress of man, and experimentalism.

Disposal of surplus goods disturbed Spanish American liberals and merchants in Buenos Aires, Lima, and Havana. Freer trade was needed, and North Americans assisted Spanish American commerce at this time. Americans carried cargo for the Buenos Aires merchant Tomás Antonio Romero to Rio de Janeiro, Havana, and Africa. Romero was a member of the important Buenos Aires *junta* of 1809 assembled to discuss the proposal for relaxation of trade, made by Mariano Moreno in the *Representación de los Hacendados*. Stores of products on wharves along the Rio de la Plata were transported by New York, Boston, Salem, and Philadelphia ships, from 1798 to 1810. The records of the Buenos Aires cabildo and consulado indicate the dismay of the merchants, while American Customs House records and shipping lists point to beginnings of inter-American trade.

Dr. Hipólito Unánue, writing in the *Peruano Extraordinario* of April 13, 1813, put the case for the Lima merchants, stating the theory of freer trade that was advocated in Spanish America. Appealing for a relaxation of mercantilist policy, he called for freedom of export, since British and French blockade had brought about a decline in Peruvian exports and prices. "It is therefore evident that our articles of export are worth little to England and we must find another destination for them; that is the United States whose flag has free entrance into all ports of continental Europe even into those of France, Holland and Italy. Recognizing this as truth, what is there to do but to take the responsibility assumed by the Governor at Havana in 1808: to permit our boats to leave Callao and take our immense surplus of products to the United States.· . . . It is very probable that in the crowded ports of New York, Boston, Philadelphia, Baltimore and Charleston one could place the cargoes of Peru products without a change in prices."

Isolation from Europe had encouraged economy within the hemisphere, and economic theories were arising in Spanish America that reckoned with new commercial need. Mutual interest was another phase of emerging intercourse. In itself it would not have proved durable were it not cemented by cultural relations and the republican system. Common commercial concern and the tradition of intellectual connection were recognized early in United States life. Within the first twenty-five years of our nationality, the major fruits of understanding had ripened to a degree that has only recently been approximated.

Attempts to dissipate the "leyenda negra" were implicit in development of contact. Newly achieved relations were difficult to maintain later, after Spanish America reëntered the cultural orbit of Europe in the nineteenth century, and the United States was absorbed in its own development. Nevertheless, a deposit of tradition and heritage had been made.

One must return to the year 1811 to find the original language of inter-American tradition. Reviewing the edition of Humboldt, *Political Essay on the Kingdom of New Spain,* the New York *Medical Repository* emphasized that, "Nothing has been a more trite and erroneous subject of vulgar remark than the ignorance of the lazy Dons. This silly cant has been imitated in our country from the English. It has been so frequently repeated and so widely proclaimed that many of our honest patriots sincerely believe the Spaniards are by a great difference their inferiors. This is a miserable and unworthy prejudice. A moderate inquiry will evince that New Spain has produced a full proportion of respectable observers and of valuable writings. . . . And as to public spirit and patronage it has been manifested in the endowments of learned institutions and in the encouragement of scientific men to an extent of which no parallel exists in our state of society. We copy the author's description of the liberality and munificence of the government as well for the purpose of correcting some of the existing mistakes as with the desire of encouraging our legislatures, associations and wealthy individuals to imitate such noble example."

Time shifted the currents of Enlightenment. Fed from common European sources, American thought was given a new direction at the turn of the eighteenth century. In the first generation of enlightenment, coincident with the independence movement, mutual relations and interest helped to motivate continental attraction. It endured long enough to set a precedent, a foundation. The structure has long since been sealed. Recent years may add some notice of the manner in which early Americans, North and South, maintained an enlightened, republican, and cultural identity.

## BIBLIOGRAPHICAL NOTE

Most of the material examined in the preparation of this essay refers to the interest of New York, New England, and Pennsylvania in Spanish American culture. To this end transactions, memoirs, proceedings, and acts have been studied. The contents of the most important libraries in the colonial United States were ascertained through catalogues. Diaries, letters, newspapers, and manuscripts have been examined. There is little precedent or guide for this paper from the North American standpoint, and less from the Latin American. The studies of José Torre Revello and John Tate Lanning have demonstrated the high level of enlightened Spanish American thought, but there is no similar measure of the extent of the interchange of ideas between the Americas.

# THE RECEPTION OF THE ENLIGHTENMENT IN LATIN AMERICA

*By* JOHN TATE LANNING

FOR those who like to write brilliantly and work lightly eighteenth-century Enlightenment in America is a beautifully bound and permanently shelved book. Enough sustained labor is now behind us, however, to warrant the tentative conclusion that almost every aspect of the conventional attitude toward Latin American Enlightenment should be subjected to careful scrutiny and, in most respects, sharp revision.

It is not true that the Enlightenment reached America only through nefarious and risky smuggling. Certainly no careful scholar would now pronounce upon the reception and availability of books in America on the basis of that estimable code —the *Recopilación . . . de las Indias. . . .* On the contrary, recent publications of Irving A. Leonard and Torre Revello demonstrate beyond a peradventure that the bibliographical avenue of Enlightenment was never so thoroughly barricaded as the statutes indicate.

[ 71 ]

It is a well-established fact that Diego Cisneros, the censor of the Inquisition in Callao, not only permitted seventeenth- and eighteenth-century philosophical treatises to pass, but that he personally collected and made them available to a few select intellectuals and then to students of Lima. In Chuquisaca Canon Tarrazas housed the library in which Mariano Moreno read natural law in the metropolitan palace itself. An effective system of book importation is implicit in virtually all philosophical discussion of the last half of the eighteenth century. The censorship of the Inquisition, well established though it was in law, in that long period between the Counter Reformation and the Wars of Independence (which included the eighteenth century) was essentially bureaucratic and ineffectual.

Yet into the mind's eye flashes a picture of an American scholar reading books tacked in the bottoms of chairs and another inserting his literature into a wooden beam upon the approach of company. This is, in relation to the whole, sheer drama. The books of the Enlightenment were read by many reputable teachers and all the real mentors with a certain mild caution but utterly without terror-stricken fear. And at long last it must be recognized that there were perfectly open and above-board methods of transmitting the Enlightenment to America. Even when the originals were not read Americans knew much about them, for the Spaniards, eclectics that they were, had many second-hand, respectable, and common introductions to the Enlightenment. That the medium was efficacious a surfeit of internal evidence shows. Jerónimo Feijóo's *Teatro crítico* (1726–1740) and his *Cartas eruditas* (1741–1760), in which the Cartesian trends were analyzed, began to reach America before the French scientific expedition to Quito in 1735. This innocuous introduction to modern philosophy and science was heralded by Espejo in Ecuador as epoch-making. To General Ignacio Escandón of Peru "the new Paladin was 'the honor of the glories of Spain' and even of the world, the beloved Adonis of America, and his adored master." Don Pedro Peralta of Peru corresponded with Feijóo as well as the French Academy of Sciences. The figure popularly called Bishop Lugdunensis prepared a compilation widely used in American universities in the eighteenth century. The *Recreación filosófica* (1751–1752) of Teodoro Almeida, advocating the physics growing out of subjecting ideas to nature, was the eighteenth-century textbook in the University of San Carlos de Guatemala. The Spanish government, when it distributed Richard Kirwan's treatise on mining in 1791, seized the occasion to distribute at the same time the new scientific terminology recently agreed upon by the French Academy. So avid was the reception in some places that the instruction was carried on by word of mouth. Hence students who had never seen the books in a language they could not always read carped the clichés of the Enlightenment. The Portuguese educator Luis Antonio Verney (1713–1792), who made use of Locke and Condillac, was gospel in Caracas at the same time. In short, if the Inquisition had been as efficient as is sometimes thought, there was still an acceptable medium for the transfer of many aspects of the Enlightenment to America from 1726 to the *Grito de Dolores*. And this fact rarely, if ever, is taken into account.

Another precaution is necessary. We must subject all people with opinions on Latin American culture to a qualifying test. To be uninformed about the state of Enlightenment either in Europe or in America disqualifies any scholar, for all judgments of American culture are relative to the European. Critics have inveighed against the thwarting of Enlightenment in eighteenth-century America as if it ought to have been in the eighteenth century what it is in Europe in the twentieth. It is never properly balanced against eighteenth-century Europe. The eminent Peruvian critic, José de la Riva Agüero, thirty-three years ago blandly concluded that, because the *Physics* of Aristotle was formally a part of the curriculum at San Marcos in 1780, Americans still consumed their time with the same sterile subtleties "with which Paris and Bologna occupied themselves in the thirteenth." This argument is sharply defective on several counts. First, it is a misrepresentation of the highest intellectual standards of Peru at that date. Second, one infers from the passage that Paris and Bologna had been free of thirteenth-century notions since the thirteenth century. If France had moved on three hundred years ahead of the acceptance of Enlightenment in America, why was it that while America was quietly accepting the new, Voltaire was asking France "to crush the infamous" vestiges of the old? Any reliable European historian will disabuse the mind on this problem.

The case that Professor Kent Robert Greenfield makes out for the reception of Enlightenment in Italy in the eighteenth century would not sound at all strange if the names of Italy and Italians were stricken out and those of Peru and Peruvians substituted. It must occasion an even greater shock to find that just as in Peru, Guatemala, Los Charcas, and Mexico, it was the Cartesian rationalists and not the *philosophes* who marked the basic intellectual transition of eighteenth-century France.

An inordinate capacity for historical opinion and

[ 75 ]

emotion often disqualifies many brilliant Latin American publicists and literary geniuses as authorities on colonial culture. Two professors of a modern Latin American university, when asked to pass on its intellectual level in the colonial period, replied in triads. One dismissed the subject with "languid, soporific, and dogmatic" and the other with "subtle, sterile, and verbose," yet an examination of the colonial archives of their university revealed familiarity with the currents of European philosophy. The first impression of the American scholar, after reading the forceful prose and fragile logic of the brilliant Rufino Blanco-Fombona on the Spanish conquest, is that he lacked the objectivity to exploit advantage he should have had in knowledge. His intensity of feeling is to be explained just as that of the *philosophes* was explained in France. He was too recently freed from Spain to feel for the late mother prison aught but a hostile passion. To the eighteenth-century philosopher the dark ages were that period when authority prevailed and the sublime Monday morning was the reign of nature. To the contemporaries of Blanco-Fombona the dark ages were the colonial period and the sublime Monday morning was the national. Yet, the Enlightenment which was well under way in America a half century before the wars of independence broke out, instead of being accelerated by those wars, was actually set back in many respects twenty to thirty years.

The Spanish colonies shared the eighteenth-century climate of opinion which sought the measuring rod of absolute dependability in the "constant and universal principles of nature." Before 1790 the collapse of authority, even that of the Holy Fathers, paralleled the rise of methodical doubt and provided the first tenet of modern science. The transition was easy enough, for the great eighteenth-century search for the super system of nature was not unakin to the scholastic's addiction to system. The Americans, taking their cue from Descartes, Gassendi, Leibnitz, and Newton, viewed the philosophical principle of authority with the same horror, if not with the same frenetic unrestraint, as the *philosophes* viewed the whole structure of the supernatural.

Despite the implications of literary critics that there was a servile deference to the *Physics* of Aristotle throughout the eighteenth century and not just at the beginning of it, the enormous bulk of contemporary vituperation against this Prince of Philosophers belies them. In 1758 Eusebio Llano Zapata strongly enjoined his colleagues to abandon all authoritative and Peripatetic concepts which were nothing more than "circumventions," and magicians' tricks to "deceive boobies and to seduce the

unwary." Dr. Agustín Gorrichátegui of Cuzco de-
manded in 1771 that ideas should conform to nature
and not nature to ideas. Indeed, Peripateticism was
a failure because it had "never explained a single
phenomenon of nature." In that same year the students of Caracas heard Father Valverde call Aristotle's *Physics* "a servile sink of errors," and Aristotle himself the "Marquis of Accidents and the
Captain General of the Occult." In Lima, the *oidor,*
Pontero y Cerdán, compared the Prince of Philosophers to the Legivia fish which, when pursued, gives
off a dark fluid to blind the pursuer. Above everything else, this virulence against Aristotle means
that nothing was more terrifying to these men than
the formulation of nature's laws without reference
to nature.

Much evidence of the acceptance of the eighteenth-century nature school was implicit in Latin
American theses. They "unconsciously gave themselves away" by an almost pathetic deference to
the natural language of the "climate of opinion"
which dominated the science of Europe. "See how
boldly," they seemed to say, "I agree with the un-
controvertible laws of nature." With monotonous
regularity we hear university students almost chant-
ing the laws of motion in Latin. *Actioni semper
aequalis est, & contraria reactio.* And they seemed
never to tire of the laws of falling bodies, the pendu-

lum, and the parabola. Thus Newton, who symbolized the reduction of nature to a mathematical formula, became not just a mathematician, but a symbol of philosophical emancipation. If it appears that he was worshipped, we must observe that it was actually an indirect way of enshrining the law of nature. "The legislator of nature," Dr. Marcelino Alzamora called him. In Lima, Father Isidoro Celis, teacher of Camilo Henríquez, added another to the long list of editions of Newton's works the repeated printing of which was part and parcel of the Enlightenment of Europe. Dr. Hipólito Unánue in 1788 published an *Index* of all physics adjusted to conform to Newton. Dr. José Baquíjano carried this enthusiasm to an open espousal of natural law in the political sense. And Dr. Baquíjano became the idol of American liberals. Toribio Rodríguez de Mendoza testified in 1791 that the students of the Convictory of St. Charles had been taught natural philosophy and natural law and had been examined in them for more than twenty years. And there is evidence that the Enlightenment arrived quietly and remained by preëmption in all the Caroline academies soon after 1767, and in many other institutions of learning. In 1793 Don Carlos de Pedemonte of Lima defended an imposing list of propositions in which Newton was eulogized for repairing the defects of Descartes. In a space of twenty years all men of intellectual promise, calling themselves "disabused philosophers," joined the hue and cry of Newton and praised him for "correcting experience with calculation." Where statute sustained outmoded tests in physics, the courses languished and the professors introduced the new in the old Aristotelian garb or taught it privately.

The constant and most reverent repetition of the name of Condillac, so puzzling at first, becomes limpidly clear once we recognize that Condillac stands for the trustworthiness of the senses. These American adherents of nature rejected the absurd "innate ideas" of Descartes and all that was not evident to the senses in favor of Condillac's idea of impressions resulting from impact of environment upon the senses. They thus reached the Lockian conclusion that the spiritual and physical man were "one harmonious whole" in nature. And so the Americans of the eighteenth century were looking for the comfortable mansions of the absolute, about which Professor Becker has told us so engagingly, and which St. Augustine sought in the City of God, the scholastics in revelation and authority, and the *philosophes* in nature.

There was, it is true, a dearth of experiment, but the first tenet of experimental science triumphed with the acceptance of methodical doubt, experiment was not routine and universal anywhere at that time, and American experimentation was retarded less by the philosophical failure to accept Enlightenment than by economic limitations. Nevertheless, at the turn of the century no imperial government could even closely approximate the sums spent by the Spanish government upon the expeditions of Mutis, Ruiz, Pavón, Dombey, Sessé, Moziño, Longinos, and Malaspina to discover the secrets of nature. The chief economic handicap was instruments. And yet Humboldt was amazed at the skill and ingenuity with which Francisco José Caldas and the coterie which surrounded José Celestino Mutis in New Granada solved this difficulty. Caldas, for example, contrived to measure the altitudes of mountains by the simple process of taking the temperature of water at the boiling point. José Moreno designed and constructed so many instruments for his students in Lima that European travelers, according to Hipólito Unánue, remarked the eager acceptance of the Enlightenment by Americans. They never tired of repeating their interest in Franklin's electrical experiments. Their preoccupation with the experiments of Priestley and Lavoisier on the composition of the air was almost constant. The *Mercurio Peruano* carried an elaborate exposition of an air-conditioning machine recently perfected in England by one "Guillermo White." This machine, wrote a contributor, doubtless with a twinkle in his eye, could be used to expel the "cadaverous effluvia" from the sepulchral churches.

Colonial officials, far from viewing the reception of Enlightenment with consistent alarm, frequently insisted upon the use of the authors of the Enlightenment in the schools. Viceroy Don Manuel de Amat y Junient (1761–1776) actually insisted that at least one modern author should be taught in the colleges of Lima and that students should be free to select the system of ideas which made the greatest appeal to them. Viceroy Francisco Gil distinguished himself by approving the courses of Rodríguez Mendoza in natural philosophy and natural law at the Convictory of San Carlos in Lima. Viceroy Juan José Vértiz (1777–1784) did the same in Buenos Aires. No *philosophe* could have been a more ardent sponsor of Enlightenment than Viceroy José Fernando Abascal of Peru on the eve of independence. The La Condamine expedition, sent to measure a degree at the equator in 1735, enjoyed the coöperation of the Spanish government. Learned societies were allowed to form, especially the *Sociedad Filharmónica* and the *Sociedad Económica de Amantes del País*. The *Amantes del País* published between 1791 and 1793 the singular *Mercurio Peruano,* which—with almost as many subscribers as the *Hispanic American Historical Review*—was dedicated to the dissemination of En-

[ 82 ]

lightenment, especially in fields of pure science less likely to involve theological dispute.

The majority of the classic martyrs of the anti-Enlightenment persecution, developed by irresponsible national writers, once we look into their cases, except when harried for political reasons, turn out to have spent their last years esteemed by the community and honored by the government. Historians, repeating the first one or each other, have told how the opponents of Enlightenment sought to substitute for the Copernican system one in which the sky was a concave canopy through which the sun, moon, and stars passed as through portholes. Father Valverde, the archenemy of Aristotle, who sought to sustain the intellectual climate of nature in Caracas in 1771, is reputed to have been victimized. Yet he continued to hold a benefice in the Church. It was not a demotion, for all university professors of Latin America resigned their chairs when ecclesiastical preferment was offered them. It is said also of José Baquíjano, who openly attacked intellectual retrogression in Peru in 1780, that he suffered persecution and defeat for deserting the "climate of opinion" around him. He had his enemies and his opposition, just as did the conservatives, but he was appointed to the *audiencia,* decorated with the order of Charles III by the Spanish government, and never suffered for his views until the situation was complicated by the jar of the wars of independence. Rodríguez Mendoza, who introduced natural law into the curriculum of Peru and prepared the mind of Peruvian youth for democracy, lived to see the soldiers of San Martín enter the City of Kings.

Now let us look at the opposite side of the coin. The force of inertia operated on the side of the status quo. Yet the lethargy which at first retarded philosophical change ultimately served to restrain opposition to such innovation. Most moderns were astute enough to blend their doctrines with the conventional formulas either to avoid disastrous open clashes or because they were actually part liberal and part conservative. At no definite point, except in individual cases, could one say the Peripatetic ended and the experimental began. Thus not only were two systems embraced in one man, but in extreme cases they overlapped in general for a hundred years. It was a century and a quarter after Carlos de Sigüenza y Góngora banished the Fleming, Martín de la Torre, by explaining the comet of 1680 on the Copernican conception of the universe, that the theses in physics in the University of Mexico presented the Copernican system as "an hypothesis." Cartesian philosophy was also "admissible as method." To scores of men like Sigüenza and José Ignacio Bartolache we know that the modern conceptions of the physical world were more than mere hypotheses and that, after all, the method was the most important thing about the history of Cartesian philosophy! It is a prime example of the opposition of inertia to the Enlightenment that the unannulled statutes of universities should enforce in certain places a kind of doctrine of double truth for a century. And, among the places in contact with the outside world, it was the old viceregal capitals of Mexico and Lima in which this situation prevailed longest and most profoundly.

Of active opposition to the Enlightenment there was considerable. The quiescent Inquisition revived itself sufficiently to disturb the tranquil and conventional spirit of Pedro Peralta when it haled him before the Holy Tribunal in 1739 to explain a theological passage in *Passión y Trivmpho de Christo*. Menaced though he was, Peralta was treated courteously during the hearings. In Caracas Baltaser Marrero, who introduced the "course in modern philosophy" in 1788, underwent sudden shifts of fortune which have been construed by nearly all Venezuelan critics before Parra León as punishment for entertaining and teaching advanced ideas. In Bogotá so celebrated a figure as José Celestino Mutis was attacked by the Dominicans for holding a conception of the universe which would render useful the astronomical observatory which he promoted and built in 1803. Although the resistance to the Enlightenment in these two centers did not triumph, there is sufficient evidence to indicate the presence of considerable and articulate opposition.

Lima offers an exceptional theatre upon which to observe the play of the counter-Enlightenment. José Baquíjano, notwithstanding the honors heaped upon him, was on several occasions placed in a difficult position by his enlightened views. The amazing "panegyrical oration" which he delivered upon the occasion of the reception of Viceroy Agustín de Jáuregui in 1780 was collected and burned. He was taken to task by the Inquisition for possessing prohibited books. Thus, although never actually punished until his popularity in Peru seemed to threaten the viceroy and bring about rebellion, Baquíjano must have been conscious of the Damocles sword hanging over his head.

The spearhead of philosophical reaction and political caution in Peru was the aggressive archbishop, Don Juan Domingo González de la Reguera, a man whose connections with Manuel Godoy gave him almost paralyzing political prestige in Lima. In the archbishop's day the case of Rodríguez Mendoza, the precursor of Peruvian independence, is an excellent illustration of the type of opposition which the Enlightenment faced in the City of Kings. Having become rector of the Convictory of San Carlos after the expulsion of the Society of Jesus, Rodríguez introduced physics and natural law into the curriculum of the institution. As a result of certain theses defended in 1787 by a student of the Convictory, José Antonio de Vivar, the Inquisition of Lima the next year called Rodríguez on the carpet and sent a document to the Supreme Council of the Inquisition recommending that Rodríguez and his students be enjoined to follow authors of sound doctrine. González de la Reguera forced the rector out into the open in 1791. Rodríguez was a man of conviction as well as boldness, for he faced the issue squarely with an *informe* on his program, which was published in the *Mercurio Peruano*. When the battle was over he was only denied the authority to offer a course in natural law. This he proceeded to do covertly. This controversy, if not aggravated by the political upheaval which made San Carlos the "seed bed" of the revolution, probably would not have resulted, as it did, in the removal of Rodríguez in 1817 by Viceroy Joaquín de la Pezuela. It is one of the ironies of the counter revolution that Rodríguez's successor, Don Carlos de Pedemonte, was the student who defended the six hundred modern tenets in the celebrated *actuación* of 1793!

But the good archbishop was also alarmed at the *Mercurio Peruano,* a publication of the *Amantes del País* and model of correctness so dear to the heart of Hipólito Unánue. It was no doubt through him that Charles IV called for a file of the *Mercurio* which, though graciously accepted by the sovereign, was an act that sent cold shivers of apprehension up and down the spines of its sponsors. And as this apprehension grew, the editors published ever increasingly banal material, passing from Pedro Nolasco Crespo's attacks on the Copernican system back to the typical colonial panegyric on the occasion of the birthdays of royalty. González de la Reguera actually withdrew his subscription to the hard-pressed publication, a symbolic gesture which set in motion a decline in which the subscription list dropped in one year from 349 to 241, thus administering a *coup de grâce* to the tottering journal. Although the opposition to the Enlightenment seldom reached the point of suppression, except when political dangers were involved, the opposite side of the coin reveals that potential repression did exist in this danger zone between Enlightenment and political action.

In summary, it is not necessary to pass upon the lethargic seventeenth century and the first decades of the eighteenth. Neither is it necessary further to establish the fact of opposition to the Enlightenment in the half century before independence. That has already been done with irresistible ease and monotonous frequency. It must be admitted, however, that two classes of conservatives survived. (1) The first class—rarely articulate—was made up of ignorant men without sufficient orientation in philosophy to make them judges of any kind. They did not oppose Enlightenment because they preferred the system of authority above that of nature any more than a Rotarian dislikes Karl Marx because he has a predilection for Nietzsche! (2) The second class, the moderates like the Count San Xavier, did not believe Aristotle's *Art of Poetry* should be discarded because his *Physics* could not be sustained in the new intellectual climate. In a sense, therefore, they were only the enemies of the well-known excesses of the century. It cannot be gainsaid that, while almost every precursor faced both the opposition of inertia and repressive action, the Enlightenment, once introduced, prevailed over the static and reactionary forces everywhere. What shall be the answer, then, to the hackneyed dismissal of American Enlightenment as three centuries behind the rest of the world?

The truth is that instead of a cultural lag of three centuries behind Europe there was an hiatus in the Spanish colonies of approximately one generation from European innovator to American academician. Even the case for the constant and general lag of one generation from the backward universities of Europe and the quiescent ones of America, however, cannot be successfully made out as the year 1800 approached. Indeed, as the eighteenth century passed, the gap became less and less. It was eighty-five years after the death of Descartes before Cartesianism began to be taught openly in the New World, but Newton was an accepted institution a half century after the publication of his *Principia mathematica* and almost within a decade of his death. The pioneer work of Jean Baptiste Lamarck on evolution was published in 1802 and was the subject of academic speculation in America the next year. Between 1780 and 1800, with fair allowance for transportation and isolation, the lag ceased to exist. On this question more documents must be read, fewer pronouncements repeated, and more attention paid to the average intellectual achievement and less to the prima donnas. In that way, the new evidence indicates, we shall find few traces of the doctrines of 1789, but an abundance of traces of Descartes, Gassendi, Newton, Condillac, and Locke. In reality, then, Americans did not so much receive the Enlightenment; they reproduced it from the sources upon which its exponents in Europe depended.

## BIBLIOGRAPHICAL NOTE

The ideas of this essay flow so naturally from years of contact with a wide assortment of printed and manuscript sources that it has been written almost entirely without the use of notes. Unessential details have thus been prevented, it is hoped, from obscuring the basic conclusions. The conventional scientific precautions have consisted of a careful checking of illustrative data after the essay was completely written. In this case such a course imposes an almost exclusive reliance upon primary materials. Of these the *papeles varios* of the national archives of Latin America and many sections of the Archives of the Indies never fail to produce useful papers. A careful survey of the archives of the colonial universities of Mexico, Guatemala, Caracas, and other institutions has resulted in a very complete collection of propositions of theses defended in the arts courses. In some instances these documents, on single pages, would have been destroyed had not the shortage of paper forced the secretary of the University of Mexico to use the blank side to record some perfunctory event. These documents, covering logic, metaphysics, and physics, are the outstanding source of information on the philosophical and scientific tenets in conservative quarters, and they have virtually never been used. Latin, therefore, is a vital language of the investigator of colonial Spanish culture.

The same search which led to the theses, however, resulted in finding some informative papers on the "volcán de la incredulidad" decrying the Enlightenment, but these alarmed harangues are the smoke proving the existence of fire. During the same investigation a large body of manuscript *cédulas* on colonial culture was thrown up. As an index to an age the panegyrics, *relaciones de méritos,* and occasional pieces are better evidence than the isolated outbursts of unrepresentative individuals. Tracts and pamphlets, when examined in bulk, are exceedingly indicative of intellectual tone. Hundreds of these, long buried in the midst of the *Libros de Grados* and *Libros de Gobierno* in the archives of the educational institutions, have not been mentioned in any bibliography. Some of them go far enough into scientific questions as to grapple with the new problem of electricity. Especially useful collections of these are located in the Archivo del Gobierno de Guatemala and the Biblioteca Nacional de Guatemala. Files of short-lived periodicals founded in Lima and Bogotá, such as the *Mercurio Peruano,* reveal unsuspected intellectual contacts and catholicity. No source is more illuminating, however, than the internal evidence contained in a contemporary book by any one of a considerable number of ordinary savants.

It should not be said that any man pronouncing upon the reception of the Enlightenment can entirely avoid dependence upon authoritative accounts. The less ambitious the work the more suggestive it is likely to be, for the syntheses have been written consciously or unconsciously from a point of view resting less upon research than upon tradition. An occasional monograph by Hermilio Valdizán or Jorge Guillermo Leguía illustrates the more suggestive type. Those authors dedicated to the more general intellectual life of the colonial period, such as Agustín Rivera, Felipe Barreda y Laos, and Vicente G. Quesada, who have not developed an argument, have tended to reproduce the briefs of their predecessors as authentic documents instead of laboring through the thousands of items of forbidding material which might enlarge their horizon and alter their conclusions. The relatively scientific works of Pedro

Henríquez Ureña and José Ingenieros are of a more limited geographical scope. Thus, in order to avoid falling into an old and deep channel of interpretation which has never been mapped directly from the source materials, it has been thought wise to avoid reliance upon these books until conclusions independent of them have been reached.

# ASPECTS OF THE ENLIGHTENMENT IN BRAZIL

*By* ALEXANDER MARCHANT

ELSEWHERE in this volume, Dr. Whitaker and Dr. Hussey have surveyed aspects of the Enlightenment in Latin America, and have referred to the state of intellectual life in Brazil. A general theme and a particular one run through their work. Dr. Whitaker, passing from the Heavenly City to a more detailed study of Latin America, selects as some touchstones among many for the discovery of the Enlightenment, first, the preoccupation of intellectual men with useful knowledge and, second, the use of academies and special societies as instruments of bringing light. At the same time (such was the prestige of Parisian civilization and such the position of Frenchmen as spokesmen of enlightened ideas), Dr. Hussey has developed the particular theme of French influence in Latin America. Variations on both these themes are found in Brazil and some of them Dr. Whitaker and Dr. Hussey have already pointed out.

Discussions of intellectual life in Latin America tend to put Brazil far away in colonial obscurity, though, as Dr. Hussey encouragingly says, to exaggerate that obscurity is easy. Brazil, so the story runs, copied Portugal and was behind the rest of the Americas in becoming enlightened; Portugal was behind Spain; Spain, with Italy, was behind France and Germany. Brazil thus appears as very much the last and backward child in this genealogy of intellectual descent. In general, perhaps, the story is true, though overdone. Brazil, following a line of development divergent from that of the rest of the Americas (as Gilberto Freyre has suggested), did differ from both its neighbors in America and its model, Portugal. The history of its intellectual life and of its being influenced by the Enlightenment is not, for that reason, less interesting.

In this paper will be treated two aspects of that intellectual history—the academies and the ideas of educated men as shown in their libraries—to illustrate the reception of the Enlightenment. Taking advantage of what Dr. Hussey has already done with Brazil, no attempt will be made here to examine the political phase of enlightened thought. Political clubs, more or less secret, did exist among enlightened men who consciously or unconsciously were imitating similar clubs in France. But, as Dr. Hussey has pointed out in another relation, extensive study is still needed; especially so, it may be said here, of the history of political conspiracy at the end of the colonial period in Brazil.

The intellectual history of Portugal, in many things the model for Brazil, may be divided very roughly into two periods, two divisions in time reflecting the incidence of the Enlightenment. The first may be comprehended between the dates 1650 and 1779, the second running indeterminately from 1779. During the first century thus blocked out, at least twenty-two academies and societies were founded in various towns of Portugal. Long-lived or short, greatly influential or not, they had certain points in common and fell into two groups. One, of which the *Academia dos Singulares* and the *Academia dos Generosos* were the type, was literary in its interests. The other, exemplified by the *Academia real de historia,* was concerned mainly with history. Despite the occasional appearance of the adjective *real* in a title, they were all private—that is, not supported by the state or the church, as were the universities or special colleges. Further, they were aristocratic in tone, for their members thought themselves the leaders of intellectual Portugal. Often they were aristocratic in another sense of the term, in that the members were of distinguished family, and often they met under the protection of a nobleman and in his palace.

Their rôle in Portugal was roughly that of the academies of their type elsewhere in Europe in their coming before and preparing the way for later societies of a different purpose and function. In language and history they did work not then done in universities in Portugal and, in doing so, appeared innovators and experimenters. Their innovations were only in relation to Portuguese thought, for they followed the model of the Italian academies and clung to it more closely and for a longer time than did, for example, the French. Devoted to language and inspired by a distressingly plantigrade Muse, they looked out through the windows of the Italian academies to feast their eyes on the landscape of ancient Rome. So feasting, they resisted the universities, but, at the same time, they also resisted influences from outside Portugal. Indeed, when men of enlightened ideas began to speak in Portugal, they did not use the existing academies, but founded new ones more fitted to their purposes. French influence in letters and criticism widely penetrated Portugal only after the *Arcadia lusitana* had superseded the academies. Genuinely scientific work in the societies grew only after the founding of the *Academia real das sciencias* in 1779 had climaxed the progression of reform that earlier had modernized the curricula of the Portuguese universities. Outmoded and surpassed, the older literary and historical academies either disintegrated or were absorbed into the newer societies.[1]

Brazil, then, could not receive all the elements of complete Enlightenment from a Portugal that was belated in its acceptance of enlightened thought. Preoccupation with useful knowledge, that happy domestication of Nature's simple plan, came from elsewhere, particularly from France, whence it was brought by Brazilian travelers and Brazilian students in French universities. Indeed, the Brazilians did not seem to have been much under the influence of the German variety of useful knowledge until considerably later.

II

How many academies and learned societies were founded in colonial Brazil it is difficult to say. Six will be studied here, four of which were founded between 1724 and 1759, and two between 1779 and 1786. The first was the *Academia dos Esquecidos,* founded in Bahia in 1724 by the viceroy of Brazil, Menezes (later the Conde de Sabugosa). Planned on the model of the *Generosos* and the *Singulares,* it met under his patronage and in his palace. Its principal work was to be a history of Brazil written by all the members, to be made up of studies in natural, ecclesiastical, political, and military history.

Unfortunately, the work that was done was lost when the ship that was to carry the manuscripts to Portugal for printing was burned at the dock. Some record has been preserved of three essays by various members: a treatise on the birds of Brazil, an ecclesiastical history, and a military history.[2] One of the academicians, despite the name of his academy, has not been forgotten. Sebastião da Rocha Pitta, perhaps stimulated by his association with his fellows, later published his *Historia da America Portuguesa,* which he ended in the year 1724 with an encomium of Sabugosa and the *Esquecidos.*[3]

The *Academia dos Felizes* in many ways continued the tradition embodied in the *Esquecidos.* It first met in 1756 in the palace of the governor to contemplate not only literary but also historical matters—historical, here again, in the sense in which the term had been used by the *Esquecidos.*[4] Here again, too, the *Academia* has been overshadowed by a single member, Matheus de Saraiva, who carried on some of his work within the *Academia,* presumably, and some without. Far from being entirely literary, his work ranged from an *Oração academica panegyrica* in praise of the governor of Brazil, to his *Polianthe brazilica.* The *Polianthe* was a work of its time, a combination of medicine and history written to describe the endemic and epidemic diseases of Brazil and their remedies. Per-

haps the other academicians produced works of
equal scope and weight; perhaps they followed
Saraiva in his other works and discoursed ascetico-
medico-critically on whether prudence or temper-
ance was the most precious of the moral virtues.[5]

The next of the academies, that of the *Selectos,*
was the most markedly literary of them all. It met
but once in Rio de Janeiro for the special purpose
of applauding in prose and verse an occasion of
honor in the official career of the governor, Freire
de Andrada. It would be a work of no kindness to
ask a reader of today to struggle through the in-
flated rhetoric of the celebration, except that he
would find at first hand the imitation in Brazil of
the literary academic taste of Portugal.[6]

The *Academia dos Renascidos,* whose very name
Fernandes Pinheiro considered a protest against
obscurantist ideas, was formed in Bahia in 1759 and
disbanded a year later after fifteen meetings because the governor of Brazil thought it harbored a
conspiracy against the state. No evidence remains
to show whether it actually did or not. Its director,
Mascarenhas, was personally distasteful to the governor. When he found that distaste spreading to the
academy as well, he sought to place the body be-
neath the protection of the crown and, that failing,
of the Portuguese minister of state.

Combining literature and history, the *Renasci-*

*dos,* too, projected a general collaborative history of Brazil and, in its short life, assigned most of the topics to be written. Altogether, there were forty effective members and seventy-six supernumerary ones. Though the names of many of these hundred and sixteen are today meaningless, some are household words. Frei Antonio de Santa Maria Jaboatão was an effective member and Frei Gaspar da Madre de Deus and Claudio Manoel da Costa were supernumeraries. Twenty-one of the effective members were priests, five were soldiers, and one was a businessman. The rest were government officials. Thirty-four priests were among the supernumeraries. A Frenchman, two Spaniards, and several Portuguese were also supernumeraries. The Frenchman was a member of the academy of Brest, and the Spaniards were members of the royal Spanish academy of history, the royal academy of the Spanish language, the academy of fine arts of Seville, and the academy of geography and mathematics of Valladolid. The Portuguese were members of the royal academy of Portuguese history, the *Congresso dos Occultos de Lisboa,* the academy of pontifical liturgy of Coimbra, and the *Academia marianna de Lisboa.* Some among the Brazilian supernumeraries had been members of the *Academia dos Esquecidos.*[7]

The founding of the *Sociedade scientifica do Rio*

*de Janeiro* in 1772 marked a distinct change in the character of Brazilian academies.[8] The viceroy, the Marques de Lavradio, acting partly on his own initiative and partly on that of his physician, José Henrique Ferreira, created the *Sociedade* to study natural history, physics, chemistry, agriculture, medicine, surgery, and pharmacy—"all that would be to the general interest of Brazil." At the opening meeting in the viceregal palace, the society consisted of three physicians, four surgeons, two apothecaries, and a practical farmer (*agricultor pratico*) ; others came later. An earnest of the work of the society was given in the dissertations on the opening day. Not only did the speakers deal with surgery, with all the branches of natural history, and with physics, chemistry, pharmacy, and agriculture ; they dwelt in particular on botany and on the profit that in Brazil could be drawn from further study of it. Indeed, botany seems to have been of absorbing interest, for the society had its botanical garden and Ferreira carried out experiments in useful botany. The academy later began promoting the growing of silkworms and imported twelve cases of young mulberry plants to be given to worthy and interested persons with full instructions for feeding the worms on them when in leaf. In addition, it corresponded with the royal academy of science of Sweden.

[ 103 ]

In 1779, the *Sociedade scientifica* was transformed into the *Sociedade litteraria do Rio de Janeiro* under the protection of the next viceroy, Vasconcellos e Souza. After some years of irregular existence, the *Sociedade litteraria* was regularly installed in 1786 and, despite the change of the adjective in its title, continued with much the same work. In 1787, its president was able to report that work had been completed by members on an eclipse of the moon, the heat of the earth, an analysis of water, a method of extracting ink from *urucú* wood, the therapeutic value of friction, and the damage done to the human system by the use of brandy and spirituous liquors. Such achievements he found especially pleasing, for he thought the purpose of any such society as his to be that cultivation of the arts from which public benefit would result. By 1794, the society had a collection of objects of natural history and what was thought to be one of the best libraries of the time and had selected the poet, Manoel Ignacio da Silva Alvarenga, as custodian. Unfortunately, the Conde de Rezende, the successor to Vasconcellos, got the notion that the society was a nest of jacobin plotters and disbanded it and arrested the members.[9]

## III

The detective exercise of deducing a man's character from his books can often lead to a quite correct understanding, but, at the same time, it leaves much to be desired as a method of scholarly analysis. A catalogue of books records the presence of certain books in a certain place at a certain time. It cannot point out the layer of dust that marks the neglected book; it cannot tell which books have become weak in the binding through much use; and it cannot always tell in what order the man elected to place his books on his shelves. Even with the limitations of this method, however, something may be learned about two friends who lived in Villa Rica in Minas in the 1780's. One was Claudio Manoel da Costa, the other was Canon Luiz Vieira da Silva.

The *mineiro* Claudio had been graduated in canon law at Coimbra and in the course of his stay in Portugal acquired a taste for academic letters at a time when Italian influence was strong. Returning to Minas, he set Virgilian pipes to echoing through the rugged hills, for, in writing in praise of a lady, he began:

Melibeu:— Titiro, como aqui tão descançado
Á sombra desta faia; não te assusta
Ver o rebanho teu todo espalhado?

Titiro:—    Ah Melibeu, que pode a sorte injusta
             Trazerme já de mal, . . .[10]

His writings soon brought him fame. In 1759, as has already been said, he was elected a supernumerary member of the *Academia dos Renascidos,* and in 1768 his fellow citizens of Villa Rica chose him as their academic poet when they wished to compliment in song and verse a new governor of Minas.

At the same time, other strains than those of academic song ran through his thoughts. As one of the best-educated men of his town, he had often served the governors of Minas as secretary, but he found himself out of favor with one of them, Luiz da Cunha Menezes, and resigned. He disagreed with Menezes, but as Menezes did not allow free expression of opinion about his régime, Claudio resorted to the model of the *Lettres persanes* of European renown. In his thirteen *Cartas chilenas,* his invented writer describes Minas under the guise of Chile, and, sketching customs and government with detachment and malicious wit, produces a picture as strange as that of the France seen by Montesquieu's Persians. Many of Claudio's allusions are lost to a reader of today, but the spirit of the *Cartas* may be caught in the delicious name under which the blustering Menezes appears: *Fanfarrão Minezio.* Not only did Claudio follow a French literary

model in the choice of ridicule as a means of political criticism; in later years he translated at least
one poem of the eminent "Volter." Open to influences outside Brazil and inclined toward consideration of the state, it is not surprising to find him attempting the translation of Adam Smith's *Wealth
of Nations*.[11]

And yet what is known of his library does not
bear out altogether the concept of him as no conservative. Out of the three or four hundred titles,
fifty-odd in law and some in history formed a solid
center. A few volumes of religious interest were
balanced by the *Ideia de um principe pratico* in
two volumes. In literature his books were shared
between Latin and Portuguese. What may have
seemed new and modern were a Spanish-French
dictionary, an historical dictionary in four volumes,
and an historical geography in two.[12]

Canon Luiz Vieira's library was of about the
same size as Claudio's, but its contents show him
to have been more aware of current thought than
Claudio. Not for him was the resuscitation of the
ancient and the imitation of the Portuguese academies alone; his interests lay in content as well as
form. Ninety-odd of his books were religious, as
might be expected in the library of a priest, ranging
from church fathers to such practical works as the
*Perfeito confessor*. Among these appeared works

in French or by French authors, but none of them revolutionary. Two by Bossuet, religious dictionaries, and other works expressing a conservative view were placed side by side with *Les erreurs de Voltaire* in three volumes.

The picture of the Canon as a conservative man is not sustained by examination of the rest of his books. He had the key to his polyglot collection in his choice of seven dictionaries: Portuguese-French, Portuguese-Latin, Tuscan-Castilian, French-English, French-Italian, and German-French-Latin, together with two tomes of the first volume of a *Nouveau dictionnaire,* an English grammar, a Latin thesaurus, and a volume of Greek roots written in Latin. Prepared with works like these, there would be little that the Canon would be unable to read.

Twelve Roman writers made up his profane classics, culminating in Seneca, the Roman who figured so largely in the writings of the *philosophes* of France. Camões, Sá de Miranda, and Candido Lusitano were the chief of his Portuguese literary works. In Italian he had Tasso's *Jerusaleme liberata,* ten volumes of Metastasio, and Tassoni's *La secchia rapita.* His collection of French authors included four volumes of Racine, three of Corneille, *Les aventures de Télémaque, Le nouvelliste du*

*Parnasse,* and even a *Messiade* and two volumes of Cordomi's *Mélanges de litterature orientale.*

History was even better represented. Two *Dictionnaires géographiques* and the *Géographie moderne* of La Croix showed him the world. For Portugal he had, besides Portuguese authors, Delaclède's *Histoire générale du Portugal.* Besides some universal histories, he had, in French translation, histories of Greece, of Scotland (by Robertson), of the house of Austria (by Hume), and of the reign of Charles V. In Italian he had Giannone's *Historia civile del regno di Napole.* In American history he had Jaboatão's *Orbe Seraphico* for Brazil and, in French, Robertson's *Histoire de l'Amérique* in four volumes. For North America he had La Potière's *Histoire de l'Amérique septentrionale.*

If his collection so far showed some recent books and treatments of recent happenings, it also showed a truly enlightened interest in the sciences. "Vernei" was present in *Opera* and a *Logica.* Mathematics, geometry (including two volumes by Descartes), physics, and astronomy were all at hand. Moreover, he had a *Dictionnaire de l'histoire naturelle* by M. de Bomare in six volumes; *Études de la nature* by M. Saint Pierre in three; and a one-volume *Mémoire de l'histoire naturelle.* But to be enlightened one could not be content with abstract knowledge. Useful knowledge, in the guise of applied science, was well represented. Two volumes of the *Encyclopédie* itself were supported by five of *L'esprit de l'encyclopédie,* and, as if this would not be enough, a general introduction to usefulness could be found in *Sécrets concernants les Arts et Métiers.* Medicine was particularly favored with Pinel and Fabri and that best-seller of its day, Tissot's *Avis au peuple,* and, supplementing them, Winslow in four volumes in French. Besides these medical books, he had four volumes entitled *Éléments de docimastique,* the science of assaying metals, and, particularly characteristic of the interests of some French thinkers, La Salle's *Manuel de l'agriculture.*

In politics and philosophy his taste was equally abreast of the new. Condillac appeared in six volumes and Voltaire in one. He had Montesquieu in six volumes, five of which were taken up by the *Esprit des lois.* The contents of the sixth are not known; were they, perhaps, the *Lettres persanes?* M. de Réal's *La science du gouvernement,* Bielfeld's *Institutions politiques,* and the Abbé de Mably's *Le droit publique de l'Europe* and *Observations sur le gouvernement des États-unis de l'Amérique* completed the list.

All told, of the Canon's 278 titles, 110 were in Latin, 80 in French, 34 in Portuguese, and 33 in

English. The rest were in Italian, were in Spanish (two titles), or were dictionaries and works in two languages and works whose listing is obscure. As far as the Enlightenment is concerned, however, there is nothing obscure about the Canon's attitude as shown in his books. Mably, Voltaire, Condillac, and Verney are all present, trailing clouds of useful knowledge behind them.[13]

Lest it be supposed that the libraries of the two friends were altogether extraordinary, they may be compared with other and smaller libraries belonging to men in Villa Rica, Rio de Janeiro, and Bahia. Alvarenga Peixoto in Villa Rica owned Voltaire in seven volumes, Crébillon in three, and Metastasio in seven.[14] Rezende da Costa the elder, a soldier and landholder of philosophical tastes, had a library that was even more literary. The *Iliad* in seven volumes, Cicero in three, Virgil and Horace and Quintillian made up his Latin. He had a moral philosophy by Heinesio *(sic)* among a few other works in Portuguese, and, in Latin and Portuguese, Genuense (presumably on logic) and La Croix's geography. Besides these, he had eleven volumes of Voltaire. Together with eight volumes of Racine, Boileau, and Marmontel and a few other works in French, his library was distinguished by eight volumes of the dramatic works of Molière.[15]

A glance at a few of the books of Manuel Ignacio

da Silva Alvarenga in Rio de Janeiro indicates the pursuit of trains of thought in the capital similar to those in Villa Rica. Silva Alvarenga was custodian of the *Sociedade litteraria do Rio de Janeiro,* as has been seen, and, in addition, had books of his own. Together with several volumes of Raynal, he had the Abbé de Mably's work on the rights of the citizen. He read the *Mercure de France* when he could get it, though he claimed that his interest was in its literary criticism and not at all in its politics. Less enlightened but sufficiently skeptical were two other books of foreign origin: the *Viagem sentimental* and the *Vida de Tristão* (!).[16]

Several of the men tried by the government for revolutionary conspiracy in Bahia in 1798 owned books that revealed an enlightened attitude as well as French influence. Barata de Almeida had a small library of thirty-one titles. Three volumes of Condillac and one of *Théorie des êtres sensibles* were followed by two works on agriculture and four French works on chemistry, one of which was by "Fourer." His interest in politics was perhaps more marked than that of Canon Vieira. A history of revolutions in republican Rome and a fragment on Fabius and Cato, taken in conjunction with a history of English America by Des Thoulles, suggests the course of his thoughts. His friend, Hermogenes Francisco de Aguilar, also involved in the conspiracy, was more interested in French letters than in French political thought, though he possessed the first volume of a *Dictionnaire philosophique* and the third volume of a *Dictionnaire historique.*[17]

## IV

Rushing through the time and space of Brazilian intellectual history makes the drawing of conclusions about the incidence and influence of the Enlightenment a tentative matter. A few obvious points may be made on the basis of what has just been presented. The academies of Brazil were until past the middle of the eighteenth century the stronghold of the literary and historical traditions of the Portuguese academies. Perhaps because there was no university to provide a fixed target of intellectual opposition, they did not early take the lead in innovation. The setting-up of academies for the principal purpose of developing applied science or useful knowledge began, so far as is known, with the founding of the *Sociedade scientifica do Rio de Janeiro* in 1772.

At the same time, the academies were not necessarily the only way by which the influence of specific French writers entered Brazil. Among the intellectual men of eighteenth-century Brazil, the ones who stand out for their originality are not necessarily academicians, though they were often friends of academicians. Toward the end of the century, both the academies and the men under French influence became suspected of revolutionary tendencies in politics, and, in several cases, academies were broken up and private individuals arrested for the possession, or the suspected possession, of French political ideas and writings.

Needless to say, neither the academies nor the strong-minded individuals perished because of the repression by the government. Political agitation, using the catchwords of North American and French libertarians, became, if not a commonplace, at least a familiar part of city life. It was, consequently, a distinct element in the discussion of the form of government in Brazil after the coming of D. João VI, if not of equal importance in the determination of the form of government under D. Pedro I.

The academies, become in many cases the shelter for the spirit of useful knowledge, survived the disturbances of the beginning of the Kingdom and the Empire. Their development followed two distinct lines. The old interest in history and related subjects led eventually to the founding in 1838 of the *Instituto historico e geographico brasileiro,* which came to have so fructifying an effect on the civilization of the Empire. Interest in scientific matters became even more pronounced than before and led to the founding of such eminently useful bodies as the *Sociedade auxiliadora da industria nacional,* the *Academia fluminense de agricultura,* the *Academia imperial de medicina,* and others. [18]

In general, then, two general impressions may be derived from looking at these aspects of the Enlightenment in Brazil. The first is that, contrary to the prevailing notion, there was an Enlightenment in Brazil. The second is a matter of perspective. If the Enlightenment in Brazil is compared quantitatively with that in all of Spanish America, it appears small in quantity and, it would seem, poor in quality. If, on the other hand, the Enlightenment in Brazil is compared with the Enlightenment in particular regions of Spanish America (*e.g.,* Mexico alone, or Buenos Aires, or Venezuela by itself), then Brazil takes on importance as the inferior of only a few and the equal of several regions of Spanish America.

[1] For the history of the Portuguese academies, *cf.* Ribeiro, I, *passim,* and Figueiredo, II, 39–45.

[2] Fleiuss, pp. 384–389; Visconde de São Leopoldo, "O Instituto . . . ," pp. 80–81; J. C. Fernandes Pinheiro, "A Academia brasilica dos Esquecidos," *passim;* Ribeiro, I, 166; Figueiredo, II, 42.

[3] Rocha Pitta, p. 329.

[4] Fleiuss, pp. 389–391; Visconde de São Leopoldo, "O Instituto . . . ," pp. 81–82; Ribeiro, I, 166; Figueiredo, II, 43.

[5] Visconde de São Leopoldo, "O Instituto . . . ," pp. 81–82.

[6] Fleiuss, pp. 391–396; Norberto de Sousa e Silva, "Litteratura

brasileira," pp. 363–376; Fernandes Pinheiro, "A Academia brazilica dos Renascidos," pp. 53–54; Figueiredo, II, 44.

[7] Fleiuss, pp. 397–427; Fernandes Pinheiro, "A Academia brazilica dos Renascidos," *passim;* Visconde de São Leopoldo, "Estatutos . . . ," pp. 49–67; Lamego, pp. 15–23; Figueiredo, II, 45.

Many writers have claimed the existence of an *Arcadia ultramarina,* to which belonged Claudio Manoel da Costa and many other distingished men. I fail to find any conclusive evidence for its existence, and I have not, accordingly, included it in the above discussion of literary societies. For the arguments pro and con, *cf.* Castello Branco, p. 245; Romero, I, 189; Alberto de Oliveira and others, pp. 300, 306–308; Silva Alvarenga, I, 48, 112–116.

[8] Fleiuss, pp. 428–430; Visconde de São Leopoldo, "O Instituto . . . ," pp. 82–85; Joaquim Jozé de Atahide, pp. 69–76; Ribeiro, I, 167. In applied science, Brazil had early attracted the attention of the scientific world, for in 1709 Bartholomeu de Gusmão carried out public experiments in Lisbon with his flying machine. *Cf.* Taunay.

[9] Fleiuss, pp. 430–433; Visconde de São Leopoldo, "O Instituto . . . ," pp. 84–85; Atahide, pp. 70–71, 75; Silva Alvarenga, I, 48–59.

[10] Ramiz Galvão, "Poesias ineditas . . . ," p. 228.

[11] Santos, pp. 234–239; Caio de Mello Franco, *passim;* Ramiz Galvão, pp. 138–139.

[12] The list of Claudio's books, made when his goods were sequestrated following his arrest as a member of the Conspiracy of Minas, appears in *Autos da devassa da inconfidencia mineira,* V, 263–265. Unfortunately for the purpose of analyzing his library, the police clerk making the list in one place simply noted that in some bookcases were so many books without indicating what sort of books they were.

[13] The list of the Canon's books, made under the same conditions, appears in *Autos da devassa,* V, 282–290. The clerk simply lumped together all books in English without noting the titles. *Cf.* also Santos, pp. 297–301.

[14] *Autos da devassa,* V, 355, 403.

[15] *Ibid.,* V, 491; cf. Santos, pp. 311–312.

[16] Silva Alvarenga, I, 139–208, *passim.*

[17] *A Inconfidencia da Bahia,* I, 107, 118–119.

[18] Fleiuss, pp. 434–456.


## BIBLIOGRAPHY

Ignacio José de Alvarenga Peixoto, *Obras poeticas de . . . , colligidas . . . por J. Norberto de Souza S.* (Rio de Janeiro, 1865).

Joaquim Jozé de Atahide, "Discurso em que se mostra o fim para que foi estabelecido a Sociedade litteraria do Rio de Janeiro . . . ," *Revista do Instituto historico e geographico brasileiro,* XLV, i (1882), 69–76. (This *Revista* will be cited hereafter as *Rev. I.H.G.B.*)

*Autos da devassa da inconfidencia mineira* (6 vols., Rio de Janeiro, 1936–1938).

Thomaz Brandão, *Marilia de Dirceu* (Bello Horizonte, 1932).

Castillo Castello Branco, *Curso de litteratura* (Lisboa, 1876).

J. C. Fernandes Pinheiro, "A Academia brasilica dos esquecidos. Estudo historico e litterario," *Rev. I.H.G.B.,* XXXI, ii (1868), 5–32.

——————, "A Academia brazilica dos renascidos. Estudo historico e litterario," *Rev. I.H.G.B.,* XXXII, ii (1869), 53–70.

Fidelino de Figueiredo, *Historia da Litteratura classica* (2 vols., Lisboa, 1917–1924).

Max Fleiuss, "As principaes associações literarias e scientificas do Brasil [1724–1838]," in *Paginas brasileiras* (Rio de Janeiro, 1919), pp. 381–456.

This is the leading work on the formation and function of the academies and societies; contains valuable bibliographical leads.

*A Inconfidencia da Bahia: Devassas e sequestros* (2 vols., Rio de Janeiro, 1931).

Alberto Lamego, ed., *Autobiographia e ineditos de Claudio Manoel da Costa* (Paris, n.d.).

Affonso Arinos de Mello Franco, *O Indio brasileiro e a revolução francesa* (Rio de Janeiro, 1937).

Caio de Mello Franco, *O Inconfidente Claudio Manoel da Costa. O Parnazo obsequioso e as Cartas chilenas* (Rio de Janeiro, 1931).

[José] J.[oaquim] Norberto de S.[ouza e] S.[ilva], "Litteratura brasileira: As academias litterarias e scientificas no seculo decimo octavo. A Academia dos Selectos," *Revista popular* (Rio de Janeiro), XV (1862), 363–376.

Alberto de Oliveira, Affonso Celso, Augusto de Lima, João Ribeiro, and Afranio de Mello Franco, "Claudio Manoel da Costa," *Revista da Academia brasileira de letras,* XXX, no. 91 (julho de 1929), 291–337.

B. F. Ramiz Galvão, "Claudio Manoel da Costa," *Revista brazileira,* II, viii (April 15, 1895), 65–73.

——————, "Poesias ineditas de Claudio Manoel da Costa," *Revista brazileira,* II, ix (May 1, 1895), 129–139; II, x (May 15, 1895), 228–253; II, xi (June 1, 1895), 293–299; II, xii (June 15, 1895), 356–372.

José Silvestre Ribeiro, *Historia dos estabelecimentos scientificos, litterarios e artisticos de Portugal* (18 vols., Lisboa, 1871–1893).

Sebastião da Rocha Pitta, *Historia da America Portuguesa* (2nd ed., Lisboa, 1880).

Sylvio Romero, *Historia da litteratura brasileira* (2nd ed., 2 vols., Rio de Janeiro, 1902–1903).

Lucio José dos Santos, *A Inconfidencia mineira* (São Paulo, 1927).

Visconde de São Leopoldo, "Estatutos da Academia brazilica dos academicos renascidos . . ." [Text], *Rev. I.H.G.B.*, XLV, i (1882), 49–67.

——————, "O Instituto historico e geographico é o representante das idéias de illustração que em differentes épocas se manifestaram em o nosso continente," *Rev. I.H.G.B.*, I, ii (1839), 77–97.

Manoel Ignacio da Silva Alvarenga, *Obras poeticas . . . , colligidas . . . por J. Norberto de Souza S.* (2 vols., Rio de Janeiro [1862?]).

Manuel de Sousa Pinto, "O Indianismo na poesia brasileira," *Revista da Academia brasileira de letras*, XXX, no. 91 (julho de 1929), 267–290.

Affonso d'Escragnolle Taunay, *Bartholomeu de Gusmão e a sua prioridade aerostatica* (São Paulo, 1938).

——————, *A Vida tragica e gloriosa de Bartholomeu de Gusmão* (São Paulo, n.d.).

J. A. Teixeira de Mello, "Claudio Manoel da Costa: estudo," *Annaes da Bibliotheca nacional do Rio de Janeiro*, I (1876–1877), 373–387; II (1876–1877), 209–246.

# THE ENLIGHTENMENT AND
# LATIN AMERICAN INDEPENDENCE

*By* CHARLES C. GRIFFIN

IN the course of the Latin American independence movement, country after country, at various times and in different words, based its declaration of independence on claims to natural rights of which each complained it had been unjustly deprived by the mother country.[1] Though far from being unanimously held when the first Spanish American revolts occurred in the wake of Napoleon's invasion of the Peninsula in 1808, this view was already clearly manifest in the propaganda of the Hidalgo revolt of 1810 in New Spain and the contemporaneous uprisings in northern South America.[2] Many rebel leaders justified their revolt on much less sweeping grounds, and subsequently they were echoed by conservative historians like the Mexican Lucas Alamán. Nevertheless, the political success of the rebel governments tended to win acceptance of the "natural rights" view of the antecedents of revolution. It was natural, therefore, that it should have been adopted and per-

[ 119 ]

petuated by the early historians of the independence movement.[3]

This emphasis on the assertion of natural rights against tyranny involved assigning a major role to the political ideas of the Enlightenment as a cause of revolution. The writings of Montesquieu, Voltaire, and Rousseau were held to be at the root of the revolutionary movement, for from what other source could the notion have reached Latin America that man was born free, that he had natural rights, that governments not based on popular consent and not respectful of these rights were tyrannies?

With this in mind, diligent search was made for evidence of the transmission of these subversive principles during the last colonial generations—a search which met with considerable success. It was found that throughout Spanish and Portuguese America in the latter eighteenth century there were numbers of men who were familiar with notorious and officially prohibited books of the *philosophes,* including the highly inflammatory work of the Abbé Raynal. The dangers to such readers owing to Spanish regulation of the book trade and the activities of the Inquisition were emphasized.[4]

Once the importance of the ideas of the Enlightenment as a cause of revolution was accepted, it followed that the popularization of these ideas in the previous revolutionary movements in the United States of America and in France was a significant means by which the fundamental ideas came to be transmitted to Latin America. The French Declaration of the Rights of Man and of the Citizen, it could be shown, had been published in Spanish and circulated in Spanish America. North American revolutionary documents had also served as models for South America. To top it all, there were the precursors: the Chilean friar Camilo Henríquez, the Peruvian Jesuit Viscardo y Guzmán, the New Granadan publicist Antonio Nariño, and most important of all, the eminent Venezuelan Francisco de Miranda. All these men could be shown to have exhibited in their writings in one way or another a debt to the enlightened thought of their time. The propaganda activities of these men and others like them reinforced the direct influence of foreign writers and provided a channel through which their ideas could be directed to literate creoles.[5]

In recent decades the pendulum of historical interpretation has swung away from the earlier emphasis on the Enlightenment as the cause of the Latin American independence movement. This tendency is the result of two major changes of historical outlook. First, thanks to the studies of Ernst

Cassirer, Carl Becker, and others, the stress has been shifted from the political to the philosophical and scientific aspects of the Enlightenment, from Montesquieu, Voltaire, and Rousseau to Descartes, Locke, and Newton. And it has been shown that in so far as the Enlightenment had a political influence, this was by no means always favorable to revolution but quite as often to reform within the established order, and even at times to enlightened despotism. While findings of this kind have not yet been thoroughly applied to the impact of the Enlightenment in Latin America, they have shaken the faith of many present-day historians in the simplistic version of its impact there that prevailed up to a generation ago.[6]

The other major change has been the growing preoccupation of the twentieth century with economic and social history. The study of economic conditions in the immediately pre-revolutionary period has made it possible to show the conflicting interests of groups of merchants, plantation-owners, and stockmen in various colonial regions and how these were affected by colonial laws and administrative practices. Marxian interpretations of Latin American independence have also appeared.[7] Other authors have stressed the importance of cleavages among colonial social and racial groups and the effects of tensions of this nature in some parts of Latin America, while still others have traced the activities of the new learned societies of the *amigos del país* type in promoting useful knowledge.[8]

Another reason for the recent downgrading of the importance of the political teachings of the *philosophes* has been a new emphasis on the limited objectives of the revolts in Spanish America in their early stages. One school of historians explains the beginning of the revolutions, in southern South America at least, as the result of a constitutional crisis in the empire in which the idea of independence had no place at all. Spaniards in America claimed, in view of the captivity of the monarch, Ferdinand VII, the right to the autonomous pursuit of the cause of resistance to Napoleon, just as the nationalists in Spain itself did. It was only later, it is claimed, as a result of the bitterness engendered by war, that the ideal of independence appeared. In some regions it was not dominant for many years.[9]

Still another point of view which minimizes the Enlightenment as a direct cause of independence in Spanish America has recently been put forward by certain Hispanizing authors. It is not based on any questioning of the importance of ideas, but rather on some new notions as to their sources. This view began with an effort to show that the ideas of the Enlightenment reached Spanish America at least as much through Spanish authors as they did from foreigners. The Spanish liberals of the constitutional era from 1810 to 1814 were also held to have influenced Spanish thought by transmitting liberal principles to the New World even though they were politically at odds with the Americans.[10]

But this was only a beginning. Of late there has been a new emphasis on the essentially liberal and anti-autocratic character of the medieval Spanish tradition. Royal authority was limited and contractual; the liberties of the municipalities of Castile did not end until the final defeat of the comuneros at Villalar in the reign of Charles I. Under the façade of absolutism created by the Hapsburg and Bourbon monarchs, it is claimed, the spirit of the medieval *fueros* lived on and manifested itself anew both in Spanish liberalism and constitutionalism after the Napoleonic invasion and in the revolution in the American colonies.[11]

This view, though strongly asserted and not lacking in plausibility, is difficult to prove by direct evidence. The same can be said about the attempt of certain authors to magnify the importance of the political theories of the seventeenth-century Jesuit writer Francisco Suárez for the thought of the revolutionary generation in Spanish America.

There can be no doubt that Suárez, like other Jesuit theologians, stressed the duties of the monarch to his subjects and denied the principle of the divine right of kings. Royal power came from God but was exercised through popular consent. This version of Catholic political thought, however, had not been generally accepted in the Spanish universities and even less by writers on Spanish or colonial law. Since the expulsion of the Jesuits in the reign of Charles III there had even been a requirement enforced by royal order on all university professors in the Indies to deny under oath that they were teaching the objectionable political principles of the Jesuits. In these circumstances the importance of *Suarecismo* may be seriously questioned.[12]

What can be said, in the light of our present knowledge, and of the various revisionist interpretations which have been mentioned, about the relation between the Enlightenment and the independence of Latin America? In the first place, it might be well to eschew any attempt to carry forward the debate as to the relative importance of ideas and of other factors as "causes" of the independence movement. Modern social science and modern historiography alike frown on the somewhat oversimple concept of causation which appeared in much of the earlier historical literature devoted to Latin American independence. As Crane Brinton has noted:

Ideas are always a part of the pre-revolutionary situation, and we are quite content to let it go at that. No ideas, no revolution. This does not mean that ideas cause revolution. . . . It merely means that ideas form part of the mutually dependent variables we are studying.[13]

If we accept this view we shall avoid the attempt to determine causal relationships. The task before us, then, becomes one of bringing out the ways in which the ideas of the Enlightenment manifested themselves in Spanish and Portuguese America in the era of independence.

What recent historical research has brought out very clearly is that the Enlightenment influenced Latin American political behavior in a wide variety of ways, among which innovation in political theories and principles was only one. Far more important than these in its effects on the revolutionary age may have been a faith in reason as the guide for the human spirit in its search for truth, without regard for the principle of authority, whether it was invoked on behalf of the philosophy of Aristotle, the theology of the Roman Catholic Church, or royal absolutism.

Faith in reason lay at the roots of a general intellectual revolution in the universities of Spanish America which was far more important than has generally been realized until recently. In every country *letrados* trained in institutions as far apart as San Carlos of Guatemala and San Francisco Xavier of Chuquisaca in Upper Peru were being accustomed to the questioning of the accepted and to solving problems by rational and empirical methods. As Lanning has pointed out in his study of the Enlightenment in Guatemala, university graduates played a significant role in the independence movement. He states:

The modernization of the colonial mind through perfectly normal and unpolitical channels was more basic to this role than any verbal Bastille-storming. We have already seen that American youth was not in darkness about any essential advance in the world. A student who knew everything leading up to and from Newton and embraced popular sovereignty could deny a Corsican usurper "spontaneous consent" and make casual use of encyclopedists and *philosophes* when they became available.[14]

A generation whose world view was changed by the study of science and modern philosophy in the eighteenth-century universities in Spanish America did not have to read Rousseau or Voltaire in order to be able to cope with the political crisis of its time. The list of men trained in such ways

[ 127 ]

of thinking and who were influential in the revolutionary period is a long one, for almost all the civilian leaders of the revolution in Spanish America were products of the colonial universities. José Bonifacio de Andrada, the chief collaborator of Pedro I in the establishment of the Brazilian Empire, was a graduate and onetime teacher at the Portuguese university of Coimbra, for there were no colonial universities in Brazil, but his intellectual formation in modern science and philosophy was essentially similar to that of the leaders in Spanish America.

Also prominent among the characteristics of the Enlightenment was a zest for the acquisition and dissemination of practical and useful knowledge. This is widely exemplified among the statesmen of the revolutionary period. Closely related to the general interest in the spread of knowledge was the effort to promote public primary education. In the midst of the struggle for independence decrees founding new schools and reorganizing old ones were frequent in all parts of Spanish America. Many of these were established in Mexico and South America on the system promoted by the English Quaker, Joseph Lancaster, which involved the teaching, step by step, of older children as monitors who would in turn teach other children what they learned. They were promising projects, and if they often came to naught it was not because of any lack of interest among the Latin American leaders, but rather because of the almost constant state of bankruptcy of national treasuries.[15]

Equally representative of the thought of the Enlightenment is the philanthropic sentiment which brought about, at least in theory, a recognition of the rights of Indians by the revolutionary leaders. In part this was a mere reflection of the romantic cult of the noble savage in Europe, but it had practical consequences. Hidalgo abolished the tribute which weighed so heavily on Indians and *castas* in Mexico. In Colombia new republican legislation attempted to create freer conditions for Indian citizens. San Martín exhibited his interest by seeing that Quechua translations of his proclamations were issued in the attempt to win the good will of native populations in Peru.[16]

Progress in the emancipation of Negro slaves was an even more important example of the philanthropy encouraged by the Enlightenment than any changes in the status of Indians. Slavery was ended during the revolutionary period in Mexico, Río de la Plata, and Chile. Steps were begun toward gradual emancipation in Colombia. The institution survived only in regions where it was strongly

workmen from Europe and in improving the sanitation, paving, and lighting of Santiago. In Colombia, Vice-President Santander, while charged with the administrative duties of the presidency, studied the possibility of canals and railways for his country and established in Bogotá a school of mathematics and of mines in order to stimulate that industry. He too sought to encourage the immigration of skilled and industrious foreigners. Similar policies were followed by the government of the regent João after his arrival in the New World. The production of coffee was stimulated by royal protection; the iron and textile industries were also encouraged. The effort of O'Higgins to do away with the system of entail in Chile was characteristic of this aim to free and to stimulate economic activity. Of course, the general adoption of liberal commercial policies opening ports to the ships of all nations by all Latin American governments was in harmony with the development policies mentioned above.

Equally similar to the policies of enlightened despots of the preceding century were steps taken in all of the regimes referred to above to improve education and culture. Rivadavia founded the University of Buenos Aires in 1821; O'Higgins re-established the Instituto Nacional in Santiago in 1819; Santander was responsible in 1826 for the adoption of a general plan of education for Colombia that provided for new universities in Bogotá, Caracas, and Quito. Soon after the Portuguese court arrived in Brazil new military and naval academies were founded; instruction in medicine was established both in Rio de Janeiro and in Bahia, to say nothing of a number of other special technical chairs and courses. Parallel to these educational institutions were the new museums and libraries which appeared on the scene. Santander established a museum in Bogotá. National libraries were founded in Brazil, Buenos Aires, and Santiago.

There is also a similarity between the secular viewpoint of the European Enlightenment and the attitudes of some of these regimes of the revolutionary period toward the Church. Perhaps most extreme in this respect was the Buenos Aires regime under the leadership of Rivadavia which launched itself upon an anti-clerical program involving the abolition of the *fueros* of the clergy, the abolition of some monastic establishments, and the setting up of charity on a secular basis in the Sociedad de Beneficencia. O'Higgins also clashed with the clergy. Santander, though he was cautious, was *persona non grata* to the clergy because of his Masonic affiliations and his regalist position on the question of ecclesiastical patronage. In Brazil it

We can not disregard the long and notorious career of Francisco de Miranda, but it is necessary to realize that subversive propaganda had surprisingly little effect in Latin America before 1808. There can be little doubt that the general reaction to the French Revolution and its ideas was strongly negative. One must remember, too, that Miranda's ideas were not particularly democratic, as his draft scheme for Spanish American government clearly indicates.

Without meaning to do so, it is possible that the political principles of the Bourbon monarchs of Spain may have helped to promote revolution in America. The expulsion of the Jesuits has been held by some to have alienated many subjects of the crown, though the political activities in this field of the exiled Jesuits themselves seem to have been very minor.[20] It has also been maintained that the colonial *cabildos,* previously in decay, were strengthened by the reforming zeal of royal intendants and were thus enabled to assume a more effective revolutionary role in 1810.[21]

We come next to the early years of revolution following the Napoleonic invasion of the Iberian peninsula. In this period there seems to have been a very sharp difference in the character and inspiration of revolts in the different parts of the Spanish Empire. Although there were all sorts of other factors involved, it would seem that in Mexico during the Hidalgo revolt and in northern South America about the same time there was a tendency to accept the principles of 1789 with little or no reservation. This was, at least, the style of language, if not of actual behavior. On the other hand, the influence of such ideas was smaller in the southern part of the continent. Brazil remained quiet under the rule of Prince Regent João. In Buenos Aires and in Chile the influence of a creole aristocracy with reformist, autonomist, but not necessarily democratic ideas was dominant. There were some powerful voices raised in support of independence, republicanism, and liberal democracy, but the general acceptance of the need for independence was slow to develop, in spite of the speeches and newspaper articles of such men as Mariano Moreno (who translated Rousseau), Bernardo Monteagudo, and Camilo Henríquez. The leader of the Uruguayan Orientales, José Gervasio Artigas, was a steadfast supporter of democratic republicanism, but he had little power during most of these years. However, if the voice of revolutionary democracy was largely stifled by the more powerful forces of oligarchy and by the rivalries and conflicts of ambitious generals and politicians, it must be remembered that the articles of Moreno in the *Gaceta de Buenos Aires* and of Camilo

ism. It becomes more and more difficult to trace clearly the relation between the ideas of the Enlightenment and those of the new era. There was a steady evolution which transformed what had been "enlightened" or what had been "Jacobin" into "liberal." Further, there was often a merging of principles which had earlier been opposed. One example of this kind of change is that represented by the regime of Bernardino Rivadavia in the United Provinces in the mid-twenties. It was highly enlightened in a number of ways, promoting education, economic progress, and good administration. It even had some of the anti-clerical prejudices of the *philosophes*. At the same time, it represented an oligarchical faction in the city of Buenos Aires which was very far from popular or democratic. At the same time, the Federal Party, which opposed Rivadavia's regime, was at once theoretically democratic and in practice barbarous and tyrannical in the character of its leadership. In dealing with this period it is no longer very profitable to make connections between political groups and the sources of their inspiration, for all these groups had been in one way or another influenced by the Enlightenment.

The foregoing consideration of the Enlightenment and the movement for Latin American independence differs from the usual treatment of this subject in that it is not concerned primarily with the evaluation of the Enlightenment as a "cause" of the later revolutionary movement. It attempts, rather, to show the continued presence of various characteristics of the Enlightenment in the latter era. A rational approach to learning and to the solution of human problems, a concern for economic development and progress, interest in education and useful knowledge, and a tendency to clash with the principle of authority in church and state—these were all manifest at different times and places in Latin America between 1808 and 1826. The variant forms of enlightened political theory were also manifested in different ways, as we have noted, in the pre-revolutionary, early, and later years of the struggle for independence. The influences noted here in brief were a part of a movement which continued for the greater part of the century between 1750 and 1850, during which Latin America, a provincial colonial preserve of the Iberian states at the beginning of the period, was incorporated into the cultural world of the West. From that incorporation has stemmed the economic and social progress that has since taken place in Latin America.

[1] See, for example, the Argentine declaration in Javier Malagón, ed., *Las actas de independencia de América* (Washington, 1955), p. 6.
[2] Luis Villoro, *La revolución de la independencia* (Mexico, 1953),

# BIBLIOGRAPHICAL APPENDIX

DESIGNED to bring the bibliographical data of the first edition up to date, this appendix includes only titles published since 1941. This list is highly selective and does not repeat titles cited in the new essay by Charles C. Griffin. It reflects the fact that during these two decades the theme of the Enlightenment has been much more actively developed by historians of Spain and Spanish America than of the Luso-Brazilian world. Among the works in the former group listed below, the great majority deal directly with Spanish America. Nevertheless, a few that deal with Spain have been included, both because of their intrinsic merit and because of the belief that Spain played a more important role in relation to the Enlightenment in Spanish America than has yet been adequately demonstrated.

## BOOKS

Arnade, Charles W., and Josef Kuehnel, *El problema del humanista Tadeo Haenke* (Sucre, 1960).

Bargallo, Modesto, *La minería y la América española durante la época colonial* (Mexico City and Buenos Aires, 1955).

Bernstein, Harry, *Origins of Inter-American Interest* (Philadelphia, 1945).

——————, *Making an Inter-American Mind* (Gainesville, Fla., 1961).

Chardon, C. E., *Los naturalistas en la América latina* (Ciudad Trujillo, 1949).

Chinchilla Aguilar, Ernesto, *La Inquisición en Guatemala* (Guatemala, 1953).

Costa, João Cruz, *O desenvolvimento da filosofia no Brasil no século XIX* (São Paulo, 1950).

————, *Esbozo de una historia de las ideas en el Brasil* (Mexico City, 1957).

Defourneaux, Marcelin, *Pablo Olavide ou l'Afrancesado (1715–1803)* Paris, 1959).

Díaz de Iraola, G., *La vuelta al mundo de la expedición de la vacuna* (Seville, 1948).

*Los exámenes universitarios del doctor José Ignacio Bartolache en 1772* (Mexico City, 1948).

García Bacca, J. D., *Antología del pensamiento filosófico venezolano (siglos XVII y XVIII)* (Caracas, 1954).

Greve, Ernesto, *Historia de la amalgamación de la plata* (Santiago, Chile, 1943).

Gutiérrez del Arroyo, Isabel, *El reformismo ilustrado en Puerto Rico* (Mexico City, 1953).

Hernández Luna, Juan, *Dos ideas sobre la filosofía en la Nueva España. Rivera versus de la Rosa* (Mexico City, 1959).

Herr, Richard, *The Eighteenth-Century Revolution in Spain* (Princeton, 1958).

Izquierdo, José Joaquín, *Montaña y los orígenes del movimiento social y científico de México* (Mexico City, 1955).

Krebs Wickelns, Ricardo, *El pensamiento histórico, político y económico del Conde de Campomanes* (Santiago, Chile, 1960).

Lamadrid, Lázaro, *Una figura centroamericana, Dr. Fr. José Liendo y Goicoechea* (San Salvador, 1948).

Lanning, J. T., *The Eighteenth-Century Enlightenment in the University of San Carlos de Guatemala* (Ithaca, N.Y., 1956).

Lanning, J. T., ed., *Dr. Narciso Esparragosa y Gallardo* (Caracas, 1953).

Mayagoitia, David, *Ambiente filosófico en la Nueva España* (Mexico City, 1945).

Maza, F. de la, *Las tesis impresas de la antigua Universidad de México* (Mexico City, 1944).

Millares Carlo, A., *Benito J. Feijóo y Montenegro. Dos discursos de Feijóo sobre América* (Mexico City, 1945).

Motten, Clement G., *Mexican Silver and the Enlightenment* (Philadelphia, 1950).

Navarro, Bernabé, *La introducción de la filosofía en México* (Mexico City, 1948).

Orgaz, R. A., *La filosofía en la Universidad de Córdoba a fines del siglo XVIII* (Córdoba, 1942).

Ortiz, Fernando, *La hija cubana del iluminismo* (Havana, 1943).

Peña, Roberto I., *El pensamiento político del Deán Funes* (Córdoba, 1953).

Pérez-Marchand, Monelisa L., *Dos etapas ideológicas del siglo XVIII en México* (Mexico City, 1945).

Porras Troconis, G., *Historia de la cultura en el Nuevo Reino de Granada* (Seville, 1952).

Reina Valenzuela, J., *José Cecilio del Valle y las ciencias naturales* (Tegucigalpa, 1946).

Romero, José Luis, *Argentina: imágenes y perspectivas* (Buenos Aires, 1956).

Rovira, María del C., *Eclécticos portugueses del siglo XVIII y algunas de sus influencias en América* (Mexico City, 1958).

Rydén, Stig, *Pedro Loefling en Venezuela (1754–1756)* (Madrid, 1957).

Sánchez Agesta, L., *El pensamiento político del despotismo ilustrado* (Madrid, 1953).

Sarrailh, Jean, *L'Espagne eclairée de la seconde moitié du XVIIIᵉ siècle* (Paris, 1954).

Stevens-Middleton, R. L., *La obra de Alexander von Humboldt en México. Fundamento de la geografía moderna* (Mexico City, 1956).

Zavala, Silvio, *El pensamiento político de la conquista* (Mexico City, 1947).

## ARTICLES

Aguirre Elorriaga, M., S.J., "La instrucción en las postrimerías de la Caracas colonial," *Boletín de la Academia Nacional de Historia* (Quito), No. 106 (1944), 113–120.

Barras de Aragón, F. de las, "Las sociedades económicas de Indias," *Anuario de Estudios Americanos,* XII (1955), 417–447.

Carande y Thovar, R., "El despotismo ilustrado de los 'Amigos del País,'" University of Valladolid, *Curso de conferencias sobre cuestiones históricas y actuales de la economía española* (Bilbao, 1957), 205–236.

Corbato, H., "Feijóo y los españoles americanos," *Revista Ibero-americana,* V (1942), 59–70.

Donoso, R., "La historia geográfica e hidrográfica del siglo XVIII," *Revista Chilena de Historia y Geografía,* No. 125 (1957).

Frankl, Víctor, "La filosofía social tomista del Arzobispo Virrey Caballero y Góngora . . . ," *Bolívar*, XIV (1952), 595–626.

Frías, R., "La expedición botánica al Nuevo Reino de Granada," *Universidad Nacional de Colombia*, V (1946), 113–178.

Giraldo Jaramillo, G., "Don José Félix de Restrepo, primer lógico colombiano," *Bolívar*, No. 35 (1954), 937–949.

Góngora, M., "Estudios sobre el Galicanismo y la 'Ilustración Católica' en la América española," *Revista Chilena de Historia y Geografía*, No. 125 (1957).

Hernández Luna, J., "El pensamiento racionalista francés en el siglo XVIII mexicano," *Filosofía y Letras*, XII (1946), 233–250.

——————, "El mundo intelectual de Hidalgo," *Historia Mexicana*, No. 4 (1953), 157–177.

Konetzke, Richard, "Die Revolution und die Unabhängigkeitskämpfe in Lateinamerika," *Historia Mundi*, IX (*Aufklärung und Revolution*, Bern, 1960).

Lanning, J. T., "El sistema de Copérnico en Bogotá," *Revista de Historia de América*, No. 18 (1944), 279–306.

——————, "The Enlightenment in Relation to the Church," *The Americas*, XIV (1958), 489–496.

——————, "The Church and the Enlightenment in the Universities," *The Americas*, XV (1959), 333–349.

——————, "Old World Background of Latin American Culture," *The Kennecott Lecture Series, 1959–1960* (Tucson, Ariz., 1960).

Leonard, I. A., "Hispanic America and Science," *University of Miami Hispanic American Studies*, No. 8 (1949).

Mateos, F., S.J., "Influencias del despotismo ilustrado español en la emancipación americana," *Revista Chilena de Historia y Geografía*, No. 126 (1958).

Méndez Plancarte, G., "Hidalgo, reformador intelectual," *Abside*, XVII (1953), 135–196.

Millares Carlo, A., "Feijóo y América," *Cuadernos Americanos*, No. 3 (1944), 139–160.

Miranda, José, "Clavijero en la ilustración mexicana," *Cuadernos Americanos*, V (1946), 180–196.

Moreno, R., "Descartes en la ilustración mexicana," *Filosofía y Letras*, No. 39 (1950), 151–169.

——————, "José Antonio Alzate y la filosofía de la Ilustración," *Memorias y Revista de la Academia Nacional de Ciencias*, LVII (1952), 55–84.

Muñoz Pérez, J., "Los proyectos sobre España e Indias en el siglo XVIII: el proyectismo como género," *Revista de Estudios Políticos*, No. 81 (1955), 169–195.

Narancio, E. M., "Las ideas políticas en el Río de la Plata a comienzos del siglo XIX," *Revista de la Facultad de Humanidades y Ciencias* (Montevideo), No. 14 (1955), 97–183.

Navarro, B., "Un siglo de oro en México. Nueva visión de nuestro florecimiento cultural del siglo XVIII," *Filosofía y Letras,* No. 27 (1947), 47–59.

——————, "La filosofía en el México de la colonia," *Cuadrante,* III (1954), 27–47.

Pereira Salas, E., "Breve historia de la literatura hispanoamericana, 1795–1905," *Journal of World History,* V (1959), 94–114.

Romero, Francisco, "Las ideas de Rivadavia," *Cursos y conferencias,* XV, No. 169–170 (1946), 77–87.

Salazar Bondy, A., "Hipólito Unánue en la polémica sobre América," *Documenta,* II (1949–1950), 395–413.

Whitaker, A. P., "The Elhuyar Mining Missions and the Enlightenment," *Hispanic American Historical Review,* XXXI (1951), 557–585.

——————, "Alexander von Humboldt and Spanish America," American Philosophical Society *Proceedings,* CIV (1960), 317–322.

Zuretti, J. C., "La crisis de filosofía en el siglo XVIII y los estudios conocidos en la Universidad de Córdoba," *Estudios* (Buenos Aires), March–April 1947, pp. 128–134.

# INDEX

# INDEX

[ 153 ]

# INDEX